ELEPHANTS DON'T MARRY GIRAFFES

*Things you should know
about relationships
before you hook up,
move in together,
or fully commit*

Bardolf & Company

ELEPHANTS DON'T MARRY GIRAFFES
Things you should know about relationships before you hook up,
move in together, or fully commit

ISBN 978-1-938842-70-2
Copyright © 2024 by Denise Schonwald

Published by Bardolf & Company
www.bardolfandcompany.com

Cover design by shawcreativegroup.com

Christine Nicole of Portrait Boutique for pictures of Denise

This book is dedicated

To all the couples I have had the honor
of working with.

And to my husband, Harvey, who has
helped me cherish relationships;
because of him, I am a better person.

Also by Denise Schonwald

Insightful Self-Therapy

*Healing Your Body
by Mastering Your Mind*

Getting Back to Happy

ELEPHANTS DON'T MARRY GIRAFFES

*Things you should know
about relationships
before you hook up,
move in together,
or fully commit*

Denise Schonwald
BSRN, LMHC

Bardolf & Company
Sarasota, Florida

Contents

Even if you cannot change all the people around you, you can change the people you choose to be around. Life is too short to waste your time on people who don't respect, appreciate, and value you. Spend your life with people who make you smile, laugh, and feel loved.

— Roy T. Bennett, *The Light in the Heart*

Introduction

I have been a therapist for over a decade now after working many years as a critical care nurse. When I started in private practice, I decided to work with all types of clients, from young children to the elderly, because I loved the challenge of having to think on my feet. I initially marketed myself as a therapist suited for clients battling terminal or chronic illness because I felt it would suit my background and licenses in nursing and psychology. I never thought, or wanted, to specialize in couples counseling. Little did I know, I would soon become one of the first names to appear in a Google search for relationship help in my part of the state.

By the time couples decide to come in for counseling, they are often at a crossroads. Something has happened to push them to the point where they need to figure out whether to stay together or break up and go their separate ways. Couples counseling requires the therapist to address the relationship issues as well as the problems within each individual. When relationships break down, something the two partners are doing or not doing isn't working and needs to change. This may sound like a simple thing to accomplish but it is easier said than done.

The stories in this book, based on my practice, deal with common challenges couples face, but none of the stories are about a particular couple. They have been combined and significantly altered to preserve privacy and confidentiality.

Reading them, it may seem hard to believe how extreme relationships can get before the partners recognize difficulties and are willing to get help. Often, people ignore red flags and warning signs, hoping if they overlook the problems, the problems will work themselves out on their own. Fear is the root cause of such avoidance behavior even though fear is supposed to create awareness, helping us address problems and make better choices. However, ignoring problems and justifying and tolerating unhealthy actions and behaviors generally results in the situation getting worse.

I chose the title *Elephants Don't Marry Giraffes* because animal species tend to keep to their own. When they do interbreed, the results are problematic. For example, when horses and donkeys—different species—mate, their hybrid offspring, mules, are often sterile, meaning they can't reproduce. That's why in the wild, in natural habitat, to use another creature adage, "birds of a feather flock together."

But among people, especially in a multi-ethnic society such as ours, different individuals often get together—as the saying goes, "Opposites attract." Even when people are drawn to others whose behavioral traits are familiar to them, they may be quite different. That can lead to dysfunctional and unsuccessful relationships, fractured marriages, separations, and divorce.

In my practice, I have seen two distinctive patterns.

1. Mentally healthy, well-adjusted individuals will gravitate toward someone with similar personality traits and values. While they may have some

challenges in their relationships, they often can resolve their differences relatively quickly and effectively. Such people are generally open to working with a therapist and willing to change.

2. Mentally unhealthy individuals, often raised in an unstable environment, will likely repeat the same dysfunctional patterns they were raised in. For example, a woman who has grown up with an alcoholic father may be attracted to an alcoholic partner because these behavioral traits and habits are familiar to her. One of my clients described it as "looking for the teeth to match the wound." Unhappy couples, in most of the cases I see, are coming to counseling to work through emotional and verbal abuse which is often camouflaged in our initial session with "we have trouble communicating with each other."

A person must develop insight and awareness of their own needs and behaviors, finding fulfillment and happiness from within, to have a healthy relationship with another person. Unfortunately, many clients I have seen over the years are unable to break through the cycle of their dysfunctional pasts.

I have had the privilege of working with all sorts of partnerships—marriages, blended families, new relationships, same-sex couples, open marriages, etc.—and, over the years, I have noticed common themes and concerns I felt could be helpful to share in this book. Relationships are complicated, but there are some helpful insights, tools, and advice I will offer to help people live happier lives, whether with a partner, in the workplace, or within a family.

In this book, we will look back and understand why our past experiences can and do, ultimately, matter when it comes to relationships. Although these experiences may be decades old, unhealed experiences can greatly impact future relationships, particularly if those past relationships were unhealthy. Unfortunately, many of the stories you will be reading do not have happy endings. Some relationships cannot be salvaged but it is still worthwhile to seek the help of a professional for guidance and support, regardless of whether you stay together or eventually decide to end the relationship.

You will also learn why some partnerships last for years and years even though they are extremely dysfunctional and toxic. You may have found yourself in this situation or know someone in this type of dynamic. Unhealthy individuals attach to unhealthy partners. Likes attract, birds of a feather flock together, and elephants don't marry giraffes. Keep these thought patterns in mind as you read on.

In each chapter, I have added my clinical assessment and diagnosis (if applicable) as well as a section offering some therapeutic advice. I hope you will benefit from it and feel encouraged to make some healthy changes in your life if they resonate with you.

However, making such changes on your own may prove difficult. Please consider making an appointment with a licensed therapist if you feel you need additional help. A therapist will listen to you but an effective therapist will help you recognize your role in the relationship and offer tools and more effective ways of communicating. Poor communication is the number one complaint I hear from clients coming in for couples or family therapy.

> *Your past experiences will likely determine your future choices in relationships.*

Chapter 1

The story of
Jenn and Keith

Jenn met Keith at the end of her freshman year of college when Keith was a sophomore. Jenn hadn't dated very much in high school and desperately wanted to have a boyfriend, someone to hang out with on campus. Jenn was Keith's second serious relationship, not including a few hook-ups during his freshman year. Keith was polite with a calm demeanor which Jenn admired.

Keith's personality was the opposite of her father's hostile and intensely explosive temperament. Although Jenn's father earned a good living, he and her mother had a toxic relationship. Her dad traveled a lot for work and when he was home, he and her mom argued every day, which was particularly embarrassing when they fought in front of her friends. Jenn's mom was the perpetual victim, confiding in Jenn on many occasions feeling as if she had no choice other than to stay with a man who treated her poorly.

Jenn also grew up fairly sheltered. Her family belonged to an active and thriving church where she attended Sunday school and Wednesday night prayer meetings. Most of the girls in Jenn's church married right after college and the rush to the altar was probably propelled by natural sexual urges as much as any other reason to get married at such a young age of twenty-one or twenty-two. If you were in a serious relationship after college, it was expected a wedding date would be the next step. Pursuing a career or staying single was a guaranteed way to raise a few eyebrows from some of the church congregants.

Jenn knew whomever she married needed to meet her parent's approval, even though their marriage was anything but happy. Keith's parents were also religious. His grandfather was a retired minister, and they were the type of family that would meet her parent's standards. When Jenn met them for the first time, the summer after they began dating, Keith's parents welcomed her with open arms. Jenn admired the way Keith's father treated his mother, calling her "sweetheart" and "darling" when talking to her or about her. Although Keith's dad was the CEO of a company, he seemed laid-back with a passive demeanor. While he and his wife lived in a sizable house, they had modest taste and were very down to earth. Keith had two sisters and a brother who all appeared well adjusted and happy. There were no obvious red flags in Keith's family as far as Jenn was concerned.

The years in college flew by and Jenn and Keith talked about marriage after a year and a half of dating steadily. Marriage seemed like the perfect next step for a couple meant to be together.

During Jenn's senior year of college, Keith lived with his parents after graduating the year before. Keith said there was no need to move out on his own, especially because he and Jenn were planning on getting married and his parents would let him live at home for free. Jenn was okay with Keith's plan. He found a part-time job working retail, not wanting to settle into a full-time job after the wedding. Jenn trusted Keith's decision even though something about the situation seemed a little odd.

Jenn and Keith got married six weeks after she graduated, and they rented an apartment. Keith had trouble finding work that wasn't too stressful for him and ultimately ended up settling for a minimum wage job at a grocery store. It didn't take Jenn long to realize Keith had little ambition or drive. When Keith came home from work, he spent his free time watching television and lying on the sofa. Keith's parents were supportive. Jenn often wondered why his dad didn't seem to be concerned about their son not working to his full potential, especially after investing in his costly college education.

Jenn started with an insurance company as a receptionist. Before long, she was promoted to executive assistant. Jenn's boss saw her potential and encouraged her to go back to school to get her bachelor's degree, this time in finance. Jenn always knew she had a knack for numbers and took full advantage of her boss' recommendation, re-enrolling at a local college to further her education.

Jenn had always been ambitious. She enjoyed working and envisioned herself achieving great things. But as the years went on, Jenn noticed she looked forward to being at work more than spending weekends with Keith which had become dull and unexciting. Jenn suggested she and Keith take short weekend vacations but Keith said they couldn't afford to spend money on hotels and eating out. When Jenn suggested a date night, Keith said he would rather stay home and watch the hockey game but maybe Jenn could order a pizza if she didn't want to cook.

Jenn started taking naps on her days off. On the days she worked, she could hardly wait to finish dinner and go to bed, some nights as early as 7:30 p.m. She mentioned her chronic fatigue to her doctor but he had no explanation or diagnosis for a perfectly healthy young woman whose lab results were well within normal limits. After Jenn made her third appointment to see the doctor again, she burst into tears and told the doctor something had to be wrong with her. He suggested she consider talking to a therapist.

Clinical Thoughts

When Jenn came to me for counseling, she was in her late twenties and very depressed. She and Keith had agreed to have a child which she hoped would motivate him and bring them closer together. She said she felt chronically exhausted and, although she was furthering her career, she felt unfulfilled. Her sadness was palpable in session and I felt the heaviness she was holding.

Jenn came for weekly sessions for about a year but could not break free of the sadness. She said she felt happier at work but dreaded coming home anticipating finding Keith lying on the couch and watching television. I thought a couples session might be helpful. She agreed and asked Keith to come with her for at least one of our sessions.

When I met Keith, I found him to be quiet and passive, only answering the questions I asked him without engaging or appearing interested in any of our conversations. I wondered if he had some underlying depression, but when I asked him if he felt sad about Jenn's feelings of unhappiness, he said he hadn't given it much thought. In my clinical notes, I described

Keith as having anhedonia, a term we use in psychology for a person who appears to lack motivation, joy or pleasure in their life.

Keith attended only two sessions. He showed little interest in working on a marriage he didn't feel needed fixing. Keith's resistance to counseling only exacerbated Jenn's frustration and unhappiness.

Jenn said she and Keith had many fights about his lack of ambition. He told her he didn't need to be VP of a company to be happy and was okay working at the grocery store. In a few years, he would probably be the assistant manager. Jenn said Keith couldn't understand why she couldn't accept him for who he was. Jenn wondered if Keith may have some under-lying depression that might explain his lack of drive. I didn't think Jenn's observations were all that far-fetched. His ambivalence and anhedonia were concerning, especially for such a young man in the prime years of his life.

Jenn told Keith she wanted to separate twice over the last few years but Keith convinced her to change her mind, knowing how upset their parents would be if the marriage didn't work out. Jenn kept second-guessing herself, wondering if there was something wrong with her because she couldn't be happy. Above everything else, Jenn didn't want to disappoint her parents. Unfortunately, Keith's behaviors never changed and Jenn was beginning to feel trapped.

Jenn didn't realize it but she carried a lot of family trauma she never healed from, too. Although it was helpful for her to come in for counseling in her late twenties, her issues stemmed back to the many years of witnessing her parent's unhappy relationship. She felt if she just married "the right person," she could be happy. For her, the right person was someone who didn't argue or lose his temper. Yet, she married someone she thought she knew. She thought Keith's persona at college was who he was. She never realized he lacked motivation and imagined he would follow in the footsteps of his father—successful in his career and ultimately dedicated to his wife and family. After college, Jenn and Keith simply grew apart.

A year after I finished sessions with Jenn, she made an appointment to see me. When she arrived, she was all smiles. Her skin was glowing and all the heaviness I had associated with her had dissipated. She and Keith had divorced. Keith had remarried six months after their divorce was final and she was dating a guy she liked very much. Jenn said after she and Keith separated, she took some time and reflected on her role in the breakup of their marriage, something we had talked about the last time we met. She also journaled about what she wanted and needed in a relationship moving forward. Jenn felt once she had answered these two important questions, she would be in a better place to begin dating again.

Although the divorce was painful, Jenn said Keith was a "great guy" but ending their marriage was the best decision she had ever made. She said she had a pivotal moment one night rocking their daughter to sleep when she decided to take responsibility for her happiness regardless of how their families were going to react to it. Jenn said it wasn't an easy decision, Keith's parents were devastated when they divorced and her mother didn't speak to her for over a month. I reassured Jenn by explaining that no one wakes up one morning thinking, "Maybe I should get divorced today." I knew it was not an easy decision to make. I could feel myself tearing up as Jenn walked out of my office, all smiles with a brightness about her I had never seen. It warmed my heart to see her so happy.

Therapeutic Advice

When I was taking classes to become a family mediator, I learned that in the first six months to three years of a relationship, partners become caught up in the whirlwind of romance. Motivational speaker Jack Wolf calls it the "lust and nirvana stage," and it is largely due to sexual chemistry and pheromones. Pheromones are hormones humans secrete that trigger a social response between individuals. Pheromones work somewhat like a "magic spell." Under their influence, we don't recognize the character traits and behaviors of our partners because we are so much in love. However, when the pheromone "spell" wears off and we revert to our regular selves, we're often in for a surprise. The suspense thriller on Netflix becomes more important for him than a romantic evening, his leaving the toilet seat up or down becomes an irritation, and her being a slob or a clean freak suddenly leads to frequent arguments.

Jenn and Keith had dated for three years before they married. Those three years were also in college when they had few responsibilities other than getting to class on time and hanging out with friends. Neither of them knew each other outside of a college campus.

Thankfully, society has evolved over the years and many of the younger generation are pursuing careers, traveling, and embracing being single rather than rushing into a committed relationship right after high school or college. Developmentally, ages 18 to 28 can be challenging. Adulting is new to this age group and young adults are challenged to navigate all the complexities that come with paying bills, budgeting finances, and figuring out who they are. The wants and needs of a young adult can change rapidly because so many of their experiences are new. While the world may be our oyster at this age, most must learn they are forced to open a lot of oysters before finding a few pearls.

My best therapeutic advice would be to wait until the mid-twenties to early 30s to settle down. Spend a few years deciding what career path is right for you and learning more about yourself. If you have had a troubled childhood, consider working with a therapist to process the trauma you experienced. Ultimately, you want someone to *complement* you and not *complete* you. The happiest and healthiest relationships are built on solid foundations.

> *Two broken people won't make one whole solid partnership.*

Chapter 2

The story of Tom and Kelly

Tom met Kelly online. Six months after they started dating, they no longer had a "spark" in their relationship but continued to stay together without sexual intimacy. They lived more like roommates than boyfriend and girlfriend. Instead of addressing their lack of physical connection with one another, a clear warning sign, they focused on their careers. Kelly was in sales and Tom was a paralegal and had recently started working at the local courthouse.

On weekends, Tom and Kelly frequently enjoyed spending time with their friends Dave and Cindy. One New Year's Eve, all four went out of town and booked one hotel room they all shared. After drinking and celebrating until 2:00 a.m., both couples staggered back to their hotel room. One thing led to another and they began having sex together, switching partners, and engaging in lesbian/gay sex, even though Tom never considered himself to be bi-sexual.

Tom and Kelly continued having random sex with other couples until they got married and started having children a few years later. After their third child was born, their lifestyle became too challenging to maintain. Kelly had concerns that Tom was not conscientious about having protected sex after she tested positive for chlamydia. Tom blamed Kelly's STD on Justin, a man she had been favoring over all the others she had been with over the years.

Although Tom and Kelly had watched each other engage in sex with other people, they were extremely jealous of one another. Tom would insist on going through Kelly's phone, and Kelly made it clear she felt threatened when Tom confided in a female family friend about their marriage. Their fighting became explosive until Kelly suggested they make an appointment with me for marriage counseling.

This case reminded me of working as an ICU nurse in critical care. When the OR would call down to the Unit asking for a "direct admit," we knew we were gearing up for a very unstable and critically ill patient. The patient had likely been in the OR several hours longer than scheduled and possibly suffered at least one cardiac arrest on the operating table.

I felt Tom and Kelly were the equivalent of such critical care patients although in their case it was psychological rather than physiological. Both were in very critical emotional distress. For them, one problem led to another and, given their complex relationship choices, more problems. They both were psychologically unstable.

As I learned more about them, I found out that Kelly's parents were very controlling. Her mother micromanaged her every decision, from picking the color of her bridesmaids' dresses to the naming of their children. Tom's father had an explosive temper and Tom grew up in fear of doing anything that might make his father angry and violent. The longer we met, the more apparent the layers of issues with both Tom and Kelly became.

I saw Kelly and Tom both individually and for couples counseling for only six sessions. Both lacked insight and it became difficult to help them, particularly since they didn't want to face the personal challenges which predated their becoming a couple.

Kelly felt counseling was helping them communicate better, but Tom told me that Kelly had the habit of saying what he wanted to hear in session. In the evenings after she had been drinking, she texted him long rants and accusations. She also obsessively started checking Tom's cell phone history. Meanwhile, Tom confided in a female member of his family which made Kelly feel uncomfortable at family gatherings.

Tom called me one night beside himself because Kelly told him she wanted a divorce. He couldn't believe she wanted to throw in the towel, especially since she was the one who wanted to go to therapy to begin with. I consoled Tom as best I could, not certain what I said made him feel better. I never heard from Tom or Kelly again, although one day I got a call from a man, who said his good friend "Tom" had highly recommended me.

Clinical Thoughts

For Tom and Kelly, there were signs the relationship was in trouble six months after they had started living together. Rather than addressing these issues, they went outside their relationship and had sex with other people, a type of intimacy they were no longer having with each other. Although couples may think their problems are very complex and impossible to resolve, most therapists gain a clear understanding of the problem—the dynamic of their relationship and how things ended up the way they did. The challenge lies in helping couples not only recognize these problems but also evaluate their willingness to do things differently.

I have come to terms with feelings of frustration or burn-out when working with such couples. I know that people do the best they can. Not everyone is capable of change. Sometimes the trauma a person has experienced has deeply affected them and negatively impacts their relationships. All I can do is offer my best help, guidance, and expertise, in my most compassionate way while accepting whatever happens moving forward. It isn't always easy.

Therapeutic Advice

Over the years, I have seen many clients who are "lifestylers." (The term is used to describe people, usually married or in a committed relationship, who are open to having sex with other people). In the past, these individuals were often referred to as "swingers."

While I support a client's free will and choices, I have yet to see this type of lifestyle work long-term. No doubt, there are people who would adamantly disagree with me, but my experience tells me most "open" relationships do not succeed over time.

When the body is out of balance and the nervous system is stressed, it requires ease. What we choose for relief depends on the state of our emotions. If we become overwhelmed by stress, jealousy, anxiety, guilt, shame, or fear, the mind will become active and our choices for ease will be unhealthy. Tom and Kelly did not recognize their relationship was in trouble, but instead, went outside their partnership for sexual connection. Later, they married and had children, but trying to build a house on a poor foundation did not work.

If Tom and Kelly are still together, it is likely their problems are no better, probably much worse.

Rev. Iyanla Vanzant, best-selling author and spiritual teacher, said in her book, *One Day My Soul Just Opened Up*,

> *Until you heal the wounds of your past, you will continue to bleed. You may try to bandage the bleeding with food, alcohol, drugs, etc., but it will ooze through and stain your life.*

If you don't know who you are, you will attract the kind of partner you will sooner or later regret.

Chapter 3

The story of
Sabrina and Adrian

One afternoon, I received a call from a man asking about couples counseling. He had a heavy Eastern European accent and mentioned he was a dentist. While it was not unusual for potential new clients to ask questions about therapy, the conversation with him felt more like an interrogation. He said he would talk to his wife and call me back. I put the man's contact information in my phone because I didn't want him to call back and have no recollection of our conversation.

A week or so went by and the dentist called again to cancel the appointment he had scheduled online. He said his wife had moved out and was not interested in working on their marriage. Before hanging up, he said something very odd, "If my wife ever calls you, don't tell her anything about me."

I thought it was a strange request considering I had never met him.

Three weeks later, I got a call from Sabrina who said her husband had already scheduled an appointment for individual counseling but she wanted to come in separately. For some reason, I connected her to the dentist. I have no idea why I felt this way other than pure intuition. When I told her my schedule was full for the week, she said she was desperate to come and to please call her if I had a cancellation. I remember hanging up and wondering what the rush was all about.

I accommodated Sabrina and saw her on a Sunday afternoon. Sure enough, she was married to the dentist. Sabrina was polite and soft- spoken. This was her first time seeing a therapist. She told me that she had been married for two years and had met her husband, Adrian, in dental school. They married only three months after they began dating.

Within weeks of dating Adrian, he began to call her stupid, lazy, and fat. It bothered her but she justified his behavior because of the stress they were both under, trying to finish dental school while planning a wedding. When Sabrina's family flew in from Boston to meet her fiancé for the first time, he was rude and disrespectful to them and made several snide and offensive remarks about her in front of her older brother. Her parents voiced their concerns to Sabrina and did their best to convince her to reconsider getting married. But Sabrina did not heed their warnings.

On their honeymoon, Sabrina was forced to have sex with Adrian four to five times a day. She begged her husband to respect her body, but he told her she "owed him" for marrying her.

During their two years together—they now had a six-week-old daughter—he kept up the abuse. Sabrina had called the police on several occasions because she was afraid her husband would kill her. He punched her, raped her, and told her one day he would torture her and watch her die a slow and agonizing death. He assured her that no one would ever find her body if he decided to kill her.

Sabrina felt a professional counselor could offer an unbiased opinion because she felt guilty. Her husband had blamed her for not doing enough to make him happy. Although she had filed a restraining order against him, Adrian had called her dozens of times one evening trying to persuade her to drop the charges against him. He told her he had been seeing me for counseling regularly.

I didn't tell her but I had never seen him.

Sabrina assured me she was willing to do the work. Before starting therapy, she never realized that she had been unable to set boundaries in any of her relationships. Sabrina said she felt it was her responsibility to ensure the people in her life were happy. In therapy, Sabrina learned the importance of honoring herself and her own needs while, at the same time, allowing other people to take responsibility for themselves. It was not her responsibility to make other people happy.

She asked me several times if Adrian could be helped and I assured her his behavior would most likely worsen rather than get better. Sabrina said Adrian wanted her to drop the restraining order because it might hurt his career. I strongly advised against this and encouraged her to follow through with the divorce proceedings. Her family had already hired an attorney for her.

After the divorce was finalized, Adrian "replaced" Sabrina—his exact words—and began dating someone else. Sabrina said she was surprised that Adrian didn't want any type of relationship with their daughter, especially because he used to use her as a weapon to manipulate her in their marriage.

Sabrina was not sure whether she would stay in the area or move back to Boston to be closer to family. I encouraged her to continue working with a therapist and told her how proud I was of her. Underneath her quiet and passive demeanor, Sabrina was one of the most courageous women I had ever met.

Clinical Thoughts

Many might think Adrian is a narcissist because of how selfishly and cruelly he treated Sabrina. Narcissism is a label to describe self-centered individuals who are typically controlling and often abusive. Here is a better understanding of Adrian's psychological pathology:

Narcissistic personality disorder (NPD) is a diagnosis overutilized. Truthfully, a healthy amount of narcissism or ego can be helpful in life when it comes to competing in sports or a job. But too much and it can become a toxic quality when the individual loses empathy. Empathy is the ability to understand the feelings and thoughts of others.

Narcissistic personality manifests when a person has an overly exaggerated sense of self-importance. A corporate consultant told me about meeting Lee Iacocca, the automobile executive who was instrumental in developing the Ford Mustang and Pinto, turning around a languishing Chrysler Corporation during the 1980s. Among other things, he said, "I am the arrow. Everyone else is the feathers." His visionary creativity was well matched by his arrogance.

NPD can be easily detected in conversation when a narcissistic person seizes every opportunity to focus the conversation back on themselves. But while one might say a narcissistic person has a big ego, paradoxically such a person has very low self-esteem.

How can people with NPD have a healthy relationship when they don't comprehend how their actions or behaviors affect their partner? As this unhealthy type of relationship develops, it can lead to physical, emotional, or even sexual abuse. As narcissistic traits become more pronounced, there is an absence of their ability to feel empathy. At the most extreme, someone who has no empathy has antisocial personality disorder and is labeled a psychopath. An example would be a serial rapist or a mass murderer.

Sabrina's husband, Adrian, has antisocial personality disorder or sociopathy.

Looking back, Sabrina had ignored numerous red flags when they were dating. She told me Adrian rushed her into marriage, a clear warning sign. He offered excuse after excuse for his abusive behavior and blamed her for "making him" put his hands on her.

Sabrina suffered from low self-worth and lacked self-respect.

I encouraged Sabrina to continue with therapy. If she was not willing to do the work to heal from her trauma, work on her self-esteem, and establish healthy boundaries for herself, she would likely attract the same type of abuse in a partner moving forward.

Therapeutic Advice

Never tolerate being disrespected. I have heard many clients offer excuses for their partner's bad behavior, blaming their lack of boundaries and self-control on their stressful jobs, lack of sleep, and financial worries. One client told me she was to blame for her husband's temper because she often did annoying things.

Red flags to recognize in a partner:

- Someone who accuses you of being too sensitive to their abusive behavior.

- Someone who controls your finances, how you spend money and whom you spend time with (including your family).

- Someone who makes you feel as if they are always right and you are always wrong.

- Someone who gaslights you (tries to manipulate you to make it seem like you're overreacting, exaggerating, or being irrational).

- Someone who calls you unpleasant names like fat, stupid, or ugly.

- Someone who distances themselves from you to punish you.

- Someone who discloses your personal information to other people about you.

- Someone who lacks empathy or compassion.

- Someone who crosses boundaries and ignores your needs.

- Someone who won't apologize and refuses to take responsibility for their behavior.

Don't be fooled by the love bomber.

Chapter 4

The story of Jean and John

Jean and John had been friends since high school. They always had a connection. Their parents were practically best friends and spent a lot of time together. Over a glass of wine one night, John's mom suggested to Jean's mom that their kids should date. She said, "John needs someone like Jean, strong, independent, and successful. His last girlfriend was so meek and dependent, I knew she wasn't what he needed."

So under the guise of a family Friday night dinner, Jean and John reconnected. The spark was struck.

John called the next day and asked Jean out for that night. They had dinner and went dancing. The passion they shared was electric. Jean spent the night at John's apartment, but they did not have sex. That would take another few days to happen. When it did, John was so attentive to her needs and lavished her with loving affection that she felt like she was in a romance novel.

The whirlwind courtship continued. They went out almost every night during the week and spent every moment together on the weekends. Jean was surprised to find out they had so much in common. John shared her beliefs, interests, dreams, and goals. He seemed to hang on her every word.

She had never felt more loved, as John continued to shower her with attention, worshiped her body in the bedroom, and professed his utter infatuation with her.

Three weeks after their first date following a romantic picnic and a frenzied run to shelter in an unexpected rainstorm, John held Jean outside his car and told her he loved her. Blinded by tears of happiness and soaked from the rain, but warm from his embrace, Jean declared her love back. It was truly a magical moment for her.

But about a week after that John started to make demands. Although Jean had been separated from her soon-to-be ex for about six months, she was still legally married. John told her that he could not date her in good conscience knowing she was still married. Jean was desperate not to lose him, as he had kindled something in her she did not know existed. She filed for divorce within a few days. That satisfied John and the romance continued.

John was unlike any man Jean had ever dated. He overwhelmed her with affection, told her how beautiful she was constantly, made sweeping gestures in front of friends, and pursued her with a single-mindedness she found intoxicating. After a year, they moved in together. The passion did not dim and only seemed to grow stronger.

Until it didn't. One day out of the blue, John pulled away and began to exhibit odd behavior. He treated Jean differently and wanted to split up. Jean fought hard to make him happy.

Eventually, they had a conversation in which John told her small things she did that bothered him. Jean, committed to the relationship, vowed to change the things he mentioned and thanked him for pointing them out to her. In her mind, it was a chance for her to grow. He was her soulmate after all, and she could not lose him.

Six months later, changes successfully made, John proposed in his standard over-the-top fashion. Jean said yes immediately, cried, and fell into his arms. They were married a year later in a beautiful ceremony surrounded by family and friends. It was a dream wedding, and they made love in the limo on the way to their hotel.

The marriage lasted nearly 20 years, as Jean did everything John ever asked of her. She stopped working and ended up becoming "meek and dependent." Controlling and calculating, John systematically isolated her from family and friends until it was just the two of them with almost no contact with the outside world. Haunted by trauma from the past and isolated Jean suffered what some would call a mental breakdown. Disgusted by his no longer perfect wife, John turned cruel, heartless, and ruthless. He chose to end their marriage abruptly and proceeded to gaslight her and slander her name to anyone who would listen. Jean was heartbroken and lost for a very long time.

Clinical Thoughts

Love bombing is a term used to describe a form of emotional abuse. This type of manipulative tactic can be easily misinterpreted as genuine and sincere because it is often perceived as romantic love.

A few examples of love bombing are:

- When your partner is moving too quickly in a relatively new relationship.

- When your partner is too possessive and wants all your attention.

- When your partner says "I love you" early in the relationship.

- When your partner acts as if you are their savior and their forever.

- When your partner is overly jealous and demands all of your attention.

Manipulative people are quite crafty. They know whom to prey upon and they are clear about knowing what their weaknesses are. Their goal is to hook you before you realize who they are and how they require you to serve their needs. Love bombing is effective because it doesn't feel insincere or harmful.

A narcissist is skillful in picking a partner who is insecure and craves validation and approval from others. This is called conditional energy. A person who needs fulfillment from others or the environment (money, fame, beauty, friends) relies on conditional energy to be happy. If their "conditions" are met, they feel happy and at peace.

When I asked Jean to consider sharing her story for this book, she agreed without hesitation. I have spent many hours with Jean over the past two years, offering her support and encouragement as she focused on creating a new life for herself. Although Jean is incredibly intelligent and successful, she has had a hard time reconciling all the years she spent living a life in a web of deception. Jean struggles with post-traumatic stress disorder (PTSD) which, ultimately, manifested physically in her case.

PTSD is a mental health disorder affecting victims who have experienced or witnessed a traumatic event. We tend to associate it with military veterans suffering from trauma experienced during wartime, but it can also affect victims of rape, domestic abuse, and natural disasters such as tornadoes, earthquakes, or hurricanes. Symptoms include feelings of being on edge, hypervigilance, and feelings of being in a constant fight-or-flight state. Others may have recurrent nightmares or flashbacks about the trauma or struggle with fear and anger. If a new experience or something triggers a person suffering from PTSD, they can panic, withdraw, isolate, or become combative.

Stressful thoughts and emotions are very difficult to process physically. Because the body follows the mind, it cannot decipher what is real or what is imagined. Holding years of traumatic experiences in the body eventually will lead to some type of illness. Illness or disease is a result of the nervous system being out of balance. This is a topic I talked about in my first book Healing Your Body by Mastering Your Mind.

Sadly, Jean was diagnosed with cancer a few months ago. As hard as she battled to save her marriage, her battle to save her life took her fighting spirit to another level. I am still seeing Jean when she feels up to having a session. One of Jean's challenges has been caring for herself, something she has had no other choice than to do while fighting for her life.

Therapeutic Advice

When clients come to me wanting help because they are in an abusive relationship, they often tell me they don't understand why or how this happened to them. Another way to understand this dysfunctional dynamic is by comparing the abusive partner to a spider. This type of "spider", I explain, works by weaving a web of deception and control around their prey. They do this by making their prey feel loved and valued, while simultaneously skillfully trapping them leaving them feeling helpless. By the time many realize it, they are already caught in the web.

As Louisa Pantameli wrote about her toxic marriage in a book called *I Am Every Woman*, describing her years of living with an abusive husband:

> *Nobody marries an abuser, they marry a facade. The abuser hooks you and slowly reels you in. Once they have fully landed you, the game starts. A game of carrots and sticks, of gaslighting, until in the end you no longer know what is right or wrong. You start to doubt yourself. You question your judgment. You question your own reality.*

*A relationship can be
dysfunctionally functional.*

Chapter 5

The story of Adam and Beth

Beth is a 48-year-old woman whom I met a few years ago. She called asking if I was accepting new clients because her husband had insisted she go to therapy. I would be her fourth therapist. The others were "not a good fit." She had no insurance and was not sure she could afford the fees, but she would ask her husband and call me back.

When Beth called again, she said her husband was willing to pay any price for her to get help because she was crazy. That sentence alone felt disturbing to me. It is not appropriate for anyone to be so cruel and condescending, particularly your husband. Over the phone, Beth said she and Adam had met when she was a teenager and they married when she was 18, a week after she graduated from high school. They had two adult children who had little to do with either one of them. Beth said she had no friends or hobbies.

I told Beth I looked forward to meeting her and working with her and hung up. Beth's upfront and brief history concerned me. Giving me as much background information as she did over the phone was not appropriate. Oversharing is a symptom of poor boundaries.

The first time I met Beth, Adam dropped her off at my office and waited in the car. When she came in, she put her cell phone in her lap and began telling me more of her story. She sat on the edge of the sofa, leaning forward, and spoke with a nervous energy, crying on and off as she told her story. Beth grew up in an abusive home and was severely neglected. Her father was a "narcissist" and was married at least five times and her mother was a severe alcoholic. At the age of eight, she was molested by the neighbor's teenage son. Beth met Adam in high school and never dated anyone else. Even before they got married, Adam was extremely controlling and mean to her. Ten minutes into our session, Beth received numerous text messages. I could tell she wanted to check her phone and said something like, "You are welcome to check your phone if you feel it may be important."

"No," she said. "It is just Adam wondering when I'm going to be finished."

I said, "He does realize this is an hour-long appointment, doesn't he?"

"Yes, but he doesn't care about that."

Toward the end of our session, Beth picked up her phone and counted fifteen text messages from Adam.

I asked her, "What do you hope to get out of therapy?"

She answered, "I just need to learn how to tolerate my husband's behavior better."

I didn't say a word.

Clinical Thoughts

Adam's narcissistic personality tendencies were apparent, but I also had concerns about Beth. I told her she appeared to have difficulty regulating her emotions, which she af-firmed, and that she had symptoms of borderline personality disorder (BPD). She said two of her other therapists had said the same thing.

Beth came back to see me for three more sessions. Each time her energy was intense and her borderline personality traits were apparent. She said one night when she screamed at Adam, he walked out and left her, which made her panic, begging him to come back home.

The following evening, after what turned out to be our last session, Beth texted me and asked me to further explain something I had mentioned in the session. To be honest, I wasn't sure what I had said specifically to answer her question. When I asked her for clarification, she texted "I feel like you are saying I am a liar and gaslighting me!"

I assured her I wasn't accusing her of lying, but I wasn't clear about what she was asking me.

She texted back and said, "Cancel my appointment next week because I no longer trust you and am going to find some-one else who doesn't gaslight their clients."

Beth suffers from borderline personality disorder (BPD), a mental health condition that impacts how individuals think and feel about themselves and the people around them. Those who struggle with BPD fear abandonment and often can't cope with feeling alone or isolated, resulting in inappropri-ate bursts of anger, impulsiveness, and violent mood swings. BPD affects both men and women although it is more prev-alent in females.

BPD cannot be diagnosed until age eighteen when it is believed a person's personality has fully developed. This type of mental health disorder impacts how a person feels about themselves and ultimately how they behave around others. When a person is struggling from within, it impacts their relationships with others including partners, children, friends, and other family members.

Signs and symptoms of BPD, also discussed in my book Insightful Self-Therapy are:

- An overwhelming fear of abandonment that causes an individual to pursue radical measures to avoid separation or abandonment.

- A pattern of unstable and volatile relationships, with emotions shifting quickly from putting someone on a pedestal to thinking they are the worst person on earth.

- Changes in self-perception and self-worth that change rapidly and are often labeled as bipolar.

- Continued and extended sense of loneliness and emptiness.

- Dangerous and impulsive behavior such as excessive spending, reckless driving, casual or unsafe sex, binge eating, gambling, and drug use.

- Threats of self-harm related to fear of rejection or separation.

- Violent mood swings which can vary from waves of deep happiness followed by intense irritability or overwhelming shame or anxiety.

- Intense and inappropriate rages.

- Excessive drama-seeking and overuse of social media to process feelings.

In the case of Beth and Adam, Adam has narcissistic personality disorder, and Beth has borderline personality disorder. Although their marriage was extremely toxic and abusive, it had lasted for more than twenty years. To be honest, there was not a lot of help I could offer Beth. She and Adam have a dysfunctionally functional marriage. These types of relationships are unfortunate because the cycle of toxicity and abuse is frequently passed down from one generation to the next.

Therapeutic advice

Beth exhibited many of these symptoms if not all of the criteria to diagnose her BPD. Although she wanted to be happily married and enjoy a healthy relationship with her children, she could not sustain either. The dynamic she had with her adult children ranged from hostile arguing to cutting them out of her life completely.

When children grow up with parents who have personality disorders, they are at an increased risk of developing a personality disorder themselves. Behaviors are learned and children learn how to handle conflict and model behavior. If they know little about regulating their emotions and developing healthy relationships, in all likelihood their personality will not develop appropriately.

Although Beth desperately wanted support and a therapist to help her, she had a pattern of finding an issue with every therapist she saw and ultimately fired them.

There is an excellent book, *I Hate You-Don't Leave Me*, about BPD written back in 1989 by Dr. Jerold Kreisman and Hal Straus. They had this to say about BPD:

Lovers and mates, mothers and fathers, siblings, friends, and psychotherapists may be idolized one day, totally devalued and dismissed the next.

When the idealized person finally disappoints (as we all do, sooner or later), the borderline must drastically restructure his one-dimensional conceptualization. Either the idol is banished to the dungeon, or the borderline banishes himself to preserve the 'all-good,' image of the other person."

Symptoms of BPD can vary from mild to severe. If you feel as if you may have BPD, I recommend you see a licensed therapist to be evaluated.

When they cheat.

Chapter 6

The story of Cherie and Nate

Shortly after Cherie and Nate celebrated their tenth wedding anniversary, their relationship soured. Nate had a lucrative job as a physician recruiter while Cherie left her job to stay at home after they had their first child. Cherie had always been the jealous type which worsened when Nate was asked to recruit physicians nationwide for his company.

Cherie described Nate as "the life of the party" to their friends, especially after he had a few beers. Nate was a natural sales guy. He knew how to wine-and-dine the physicians, but Cherie often questioned his tactics, especially when she called him late at night and it was obvious to her that he was still out and about. Nate's loud and obnoxious frat boy tone made her skin crawl. She couldn't help but wonder whether Nate ever crossed any lines.

One evening, Nate was packing to go up to New York on business. Cherie felt something was off and she had a gut feeling she should check Nate's phone. After he had packed his suitcase, Nate headed into the shower and Cherie nonchalantly grabbed his phone and went into the kitchen. She noticed he had been on Facebook messenger quite a bit and took a screenshot of his activity with "Dawn," whom she said looked vaguely familiar to her at first glance.

After taking several screenshots, Cherie went into their walk-in closet to read Nate's messages and to see what the heck was going on. While she was at it, she pulled up Dawn's profile and recognized her as someone they both knew in college. Cherie had no idea Nate had any contact with her over the years. Not only had they connected, they were planning on meeting up in New York. It turned out that over the past few months, Nate and Dawn had exchanged dozens of sexually graphic pictures and messages about what they were going to do to each other when they could finally be alone.

Cherie lost it. She stormed into the bathroom, ripped open the shower curtain, and said, "I can't believe you would do this to us. You are a pathetic asshole and I am done with this marriage!"

Nate grabbed a towel and told Cherie he had no idea what she was talking about.

In response, she began reading Dawn's texts: "I always thought you were hot and am surprised we never hooked up back in college." The more she read, the more Nate knew there was nothing he could say other than "I'm sorry" and "Please forgive me" but there wasn't anything he could say that would appease Cherie. Desperate, Nate said he would do anything to save the marriage and promised that he would find them a marriage counselor to help.

When Nate called me at 8:00 a.m. that Monday morning, he had not slept and I could hear the anguish in his voice. "We need marriage counseling as soon as you can get us in," he begged.

I suggested an appointment that Friday but he said the marriage wasn't going to make it that long. "How about today at 5:00 p.m.?" I offered. He let out a sigh of relief and took down my office address. He said if his insurance didn't cover it, he would pay out-of-pocket regardless of how much it cost. He never asked how much that would be.

When Cherie and Nate came to my office, she was dressed as if she were going out to a club or a nice dinner afterward. Her make-up was impeccably applied and it looked like she had spent a long time fixing her hair. Nate looked rough, to say the least. He was wearing sweatpants, his face was unshaven, and his eyes were puffy as if he had been crying.

After we all introduced ourselves, I suggested I start by asking them a few questions. The tension in the room was thick enough to cut with a knife, and because I needed to get their history anyway, I felt it might be a good icebreaker. Nate was a big guy and as they sat on the loveseat in my office, Cherie made sure there was an adequate amount of space in between them. She softened slightly when my therapy dog, Henry, put his paw on her leg hoping she was going to pet him.

After Cherie and Nate had answered all my questions very matter-of-factly, I said, "Who would like to start to tell me why you are here and how I might be able to help?"

Cherie gave Nate a snide, annoyed look and said, "Go ahead."

Nate burst into tears. He said he had been unfaithful and was having an emotional affair because the pressures of his job had become overwhelming for him.

Cherie rolled her eyes and said "Yeah, it's your job that caused all this. Give me a break!"

Nate said he worked in sales and traveled a lot for business which ultimately led to heavy drinking with his clients. The camaraderie and alcohol were a good combination to get the doctors to "sign on the dotted line" by the end of the night.

Cherie rolled her eyes at him again. Then, she chimed in to tell me that Nate's drinking had been an ongoing problem. "Nate loves to be the life of the party," she said. "When he drinks, he drinks to excess and tends to be loud and obnoxious. When he is traveling, I call and text him numerous times on the evenings he is out of town to make sure he isn't plastered by 10:00 p.m. and is back in his room at a decent time." Thinking back, Cherie said Nate probably has had numerous girlfriends and it wasn't hard to connect the dots after she thought back to his erratic behavior over the years.

Nate became defensive and assured me he did enjoy drinking but he was not an alcoholic. He also denied any inappropriateness outside the marriage but Cherie wasn't buying any of it.

Cherie said, "Then why did you snort cocaine if you weren't drunk that one time in Dallas?"

Nate admitted he had tried cocaine once on a business trip to Dallas a while back which caused him to have a panic attack. It freaked him out and he never tried it again.

Cherie said she had spent all day confiding in her girlfriend who told her she should get a divorce. Her girlfriend had the same thing happen to her five years ago and said she regretted not leaving her husband back then. Nate assured Cherie he would do whatever it took to change and I witnessed that big strapping guy, sitting in front of me, fall to pieces as he wept like a baby.

Clinical Thoughts

No matter how wonderful our lives may be, we all experience stress. We have work stress, relationship stress, children stress, financial stress; the list goes on and on. When the body is stressed, it requires balance and relief. As I mentioned earlier, because the body is cued by the mind, an unhealthy anxious mind can cause the body to become distressed. If our thoughts and emotions, such as worry, guilt, and control, are fear-based, the mind will become extremely active. When this happens, it will often create some unhealthy coping mechanisms which, if we are not careful, can lead to addiction, including smoking, drinking, gambling, pornography, and getting high.

I have noticed that among men who work in highly stressful jobs, it is not unusual for them to turn to some form of sexual relief, often in the form of pornography, extramarital affairs, visits to massage parlors, or emotional affairs. I have met with male clients who have had emotional affairs with women for many years, despite the fact they have never met each other in person. Typically, I see women turn more to food or alcohol.

Social media is another way for both men and women to numb their feelings and cope with stress. Unfortunately, social media can be a double-edged sword. While many people use it to distract them, it can cause an increase in anxiety, procrastination, and depression because it over-stimulates the mind.

As our weekly sessions progressed, Cherie said she had spent hours checking up on Nate. She tracked his phone and checked his email and messages daily. She was petrified he would cheat on her again. During one session I asked Cherie if this was how she wanted to spend her life, obsessing over whether her husband was going to remain faithful to her. I even suggested if she could not bring herself to trust him ever again, perhaps she should decide whether to stay in the marriage.

Cherie was well educated and although she was a stay-at-home mom, she could easily go back to work and support herself. She said she wanted to stay married but, at the same time, she felt the need to "control" the situation. As therapists, helping clients give up the need to control, worry, or feel guilty is among our greatest challenges. All of these feelings are extremely harmful to the body and mind.

Cherie and Nate came in for weekly therapy sessions for about six weeks until Nate texted me one evening asking me to cancel an upcoming appointment. He said Cherie had been admitted to the hospital with severe diverticulitis and sepsis and she was being transferred to the ICU. After a week or so had passed, I texted Nate to ask how Cherie was feeling but never got a response. I put a "get well" card to Cherie in the mail but never heard from her either.

The more I thought back to our sessions, it was obvious Nate was going through the motions, losing momentum as the weeks went on. He said several times, "I don't know what else you want me to do in order for you to move past all this."

Cherie felt it was her responsibility to control the situation. But control is a myth. Trying to control something is like trying to rein in the wind. Although we cannot control what happens to us, we can control our perception of it. We also can make choices. Life happens for us and not to us. Every situation is a chance to grow and learn. When we can find lessons and meanings behind tough times, they lose their sting and the pain will lessen. Cherie had a choice and she chose to stay in the mind-energy of the problem and continue to suffer. At least that's what she was doing the last time we met. It was sad to hear Cherie had become so sick but, unfortunately, her body was paying the price.

Therapeutic Advice:

It is important to define what you will and will not tolerate in a relationship. If your partner is not faithful, are you willing to forgive and move forward? If your partner is not respectful to you, are you willing to tolerate it? If your partner is dismissive of your needs, will you be able to live with it? If the answer to any of these questions is "No," then you need to be willing to walk away. If you choose to stay and ignore your "inner knowing," you will never feel at peace, and your health will decline as a result.

I have seen several clients over the years who have chosen to stay in their relationship after their partner has been unfaithful. Yet, many of them have struggled to move forward without holding a tremendous amount of bitterness and resentment. Bitterness and resentment are low vibrational energies that cause energy to block around the heart. Over time, this can manifest through heart problems, high blood pressure (hypertension), lung problems, and breast cancer in women. Anger is another culprit for these types of health issues.

My advice for a person in such a situation is to decide if you are willing to forgive your partner for betraying you, hurting you, and causing you pain. Truth be told, there are times we need others to forgive us because we, ourselves, are not

Schonwald

perfect either. But, if in your heart of hearts, you cannot forget and cannot forgive, you need to move on. Holding your partner accountable for something they cannot take back is unfair and can never be resolved. In the end, you are not honoring them and you are not honoring yourself.

It is possible to forgive your partner and move forward into a happy and healthy relationship but it takes work. The work comes from within. In Cherie's case, she chose to move forward fearfully and took it upon herself to make sure Nate didn't cheat. That same amount of energy could have been spent on working on her fears and insecurities while focusing more on building a healthier relationship with Nate.

Be clear with yourself about what you have to offer and what you want before you look for a partner.

Chapter 7

The story of Sarah and Joe

Sarah was a 47-year-old chief financial officer at a very successful company and had been married for 17 years. She had met her husband, Joe, in college where he was majoring in engineering. They married after graduation and had a baby girl a year later. Within a year after their daughter was born, Sarah gave birth to a son.

Because Sarah earned a healthy salary, Joe felt it was best to stay home with the children and manage the household. Little by little, he took it upon himself to make every and all decisions regarding finances, the children, and even little things such as how much Sarah was allowed to spend at the hair salon or buying clothes.

Sarah said it was easier to give Joe full control rather than speak up and deal with his explosive temper. She said every week, he reviewed her credit card charges to make sure she had not exceeded the budget he had allotted for her. When Joe questioned Sarah, she felt overwhelmed with guilt and anxiety. She said her goal was to raise their children in a normal environment and didn't want them to be exposed to any tension in their home. She looked forward to a glass or two of wine in the evenings, the only thing that seemed to help consistently calm her nerves.

Sarah preferred going to work where she felt more comfortable with her colleagues than with her husband. There she met Jason, who had started as a summer intern in her firm. Jason was engaging and thoughtful. He was an avid reader and connected with Sarah the first day she met him, complimenting her on the artwork in her office and the necklace she wore, which her mother gave her for her college graduation present.

Jason was easy to talk to and, at some point, Sarah confided in him about her troubled marriage. Jason told Sarah he had seen a therapist after breaking up with his girlfriend and felt therapy might be helpful for her. Sarah wasn't sure Joe would allow her to spend money on that but was relieved to learn her insurance would cover the cost. If she blocked out time for a "meeting" on her schedule, she could slip out for an hour without raising any concerns among the staff or, more importantly, Joe.

Sarah scheduled an appointment on a Tuesday afternoon in my office and said Jason had referred her. I remembered Jason even though I had only met him twice. I wondered how they knew each other but didn't ask.

As Sarah shared her story, she couldn't hold back the tears. She felt trapped and suffocated in her marriage and wanted to leave Joe but couldn't see a way out. She talked about her overwhelming anxiety and her drinking. She said," I know I shouldn't use alcohol as a coping mechanism but it is the only thing I have available because I refuse to take medication."

By our third session, Sarah said coming to counseling had helped her immensely and told me she and Jason were having an affair. They had a deep connection and having him in her life helped her tolerate the tyrant of a husband she had waiting for her at home. Joe's micromanaging did not let up and the children were starting to notice that Dad was often in a bad mood and mad about things.

The more I met with Sarah, the more impressed I was with her. She was intelligent, articulate, and had a sweet personality. I remember wondering how she would answer an important question, "What do you bring to the table in a relationship?"

"What do you mean?" she said.

"Okay, let me ask this in a different way," I elaborated. "What do you offer to your company that makes you so valuable?"

She went on for several minutes about how she earned her way to the top, starting with attending a prestigious college, coupled with discipline and a lot of hard work. Sarah read several motivational books that influenced her and contributed to her success. Her favorite was *The Four Agreements* by Don Miguel Ruiz, a Mexican author and spiritual teacher whose mother was a healer and grandfather was a shaman. The book posits a code of honor to live by based on ancient Toltec beliefs:

1. Be impeccable with your word.
2. Don't take anything personally.
3. Don't make assumptions.
4. Always do your best.

I told Sarah I loved the book too—it had been life-changing for me as well—and I had recommended it to several of my patients.

I continued that it was obvious to me how Sarah became so successful. What I didn't understand was why she allowed herself to tolerate financial and emotional abuse from her husband in her personal life.

Sarah burst into tears. "I don't know, that's what I thought I deserved," She said.

To all appearances, Sarah was very successful in her career, but underneath that façade, she suffered from low self-worth.

A few examples of self-respect are:

- Honoring your needs.

- Speaking up and setting limits about how you want to be treated.

- Making choices you feel comfortable with.

- Practicing self-love including exercising, eating properly, sleeping, going to the doctor, etc.

- Honoring your word, avoiding people-pleasing.

- Being on time and honoring your commitments.

Signs and symptoms of low self-worth are inability to set personal boundaries, people pleasing, negative self-talk, unresolved trauma, tolerating abusive behavior, neglecting or not prioritizing your own needs.

Sarah was offered a big promotion by her firm and transferred out west to California. She had the courage to ask Joe for a divorce and texted me to tell me he had taken her to the cleaners financially but it was worth it. Joe also had moved to California because they shared custody of the children and it was the only way he would be willing to let her move. Sarah said she had hoped they could successfully co-parent someday.

I told her I was not sure that would happen but it would be wonderful if it did. She had hoped Joe would find a job and start dating but hadn't done either the last time we spoke.

Sarah said she wanted to find a therapist in California and continue counseling but felt it would be better for her to find someone near her and be seen in person. I wished her well and asked her to keep in touch.

Clinical Thoughts

Sometimes, the personality traits and tendencies of a person who suffers from narcissistic personality disorder are downright shocking! There doesn't seem to be any line they won't cross ranging from financial control to isolating their partner from their family and friends. But, never in my wildest dreams would I have predicted the outcome of this case.

As Sarah began to liberate herself from Joe, his behavior became more extreme and radical. What I have experienced over the years is that narcissists are generally not fond of their partner coming for therapy. Many of my clients have told me after our session together, their partner insisted they repeat everything we talked about in the session. On occasion, the narcissistic partner will call me and "set the record straight" wanting me to know their partner has a lot of issues and they are really the victims. When I suggest they make an appointment to come in and meet with me in person, they are curt and frequently dismissive.

By now, you probably recognize Joe as another example of an over-controlling narcissist. A few examples of Joe's narcissistic and controlling manipulation tactics were:

• Micromanaging and badgering Sara to get his way.

- Joe's explosive temperament.

- Joe's shaming and humiliation by making her adhere to a tight budget.

- Financial abuse by micromanaging her spending and assigning Sara a limit to what she was allowed to spend on her hair and clothes.

The overall theme of the narcissist is power and control. The love bombing we talked about earlier is deceiving because it is mistaken for true love. The web of a narcissist can feel inescapable to the person caught because they are made to feel there is no way out. In Sarah's case, she was the breadwinner and earned an excellent salary. Yet, she remained stuck in an emotionally abusive marriage for many years until she finally mustered the courage to leave. What she didn't realize was all those years of pacifying Joe made him go to violent measures to control her fate. Yet, never would I have imagined what would happen next.

Three months later, I got a text one night from my office manager. She said she saw Sarah's name on the news. Her ex-husband had murdered her and then shot himself. When the police arrived, they found the children huddled in the closet.

These are the cases a therapist never forgets. I can remember reading the text, putting my head in my hands, and crying hysterically. People often ask me how I handle being a therapist. That night, I didn't handle it very well at all.

Therapeutic Advice

This case was heart-wrenching. In hindsight, there were a lot of red flags Sarah overlooked: Joe's controlling behavior, the financial abuse, and his explosive temper. All of these pointed to a potentially dangerous situation. In Sarah's case, these oversights led to a tragic outcome.

Not all who divorce narcissistic partners fear for their lives or are at risk of being murdered. This is an extreme case but, as a therapist, this type of shocking ending is not far-fetched. I never underestimate what a narcissistic personality is capable of. Some lack courage and will back down when confronted. Others go to the extreme, become violent, and drag out their legal battles with their spouses for years, many times using the children as pawns. Then there are the rare cases that end tragically, as Sarah's did, which are difficult for even a trained therapist to fathom.

The craving for power and control of a narcissist is insatiable. It is like taking a full pitcher of water and pouring it into a pot that has a hole in the bottom. You can never fill it. Narcissistic people need external power, something outside of themselves and often in the environment, such as money, prestige, sex, and validation to feel satisfied. But these feelings of "satisfaction" are fleeting.

Many women enter relationships believing they can change their spouse over time, but this runs counter to centuries of human experience. There is an old joke: "How many therapists does it take to change a lightbulb? Only one, but the lightbulb must want to change." It is the naive individual who believes they can fix other people.

If you are in an abusive relationship and need help, help is available. Call the National Domestic Violence Hotline for support, resources, and advice. Call 1-800-SAFE (7233). Help is available for you 24/7.

> *It doesn't matter why*
> *you attract the wrong person.*
> *It matters that you do.*

Chapter 8

The story of
Sandy and Deanna

Sandy was the realtor for Deanna and Becky, who helped the couple purchase a home after they moved from Denver to the east coast of Florida. Becky had a good job working for the government which allowed her to work remotely. Becky earned a healthy salary and Deanna hadn't worked full-time in years.

Sandy had been single for almost three years. She and her girlfriend, Pam, had ended their fifteen-year relationship and Sandy was finally feeling financially stable on her own. The real estate market was thriving and she had a part-time job working as a bartender on the weekends.

Because Becky worked long hours, Deanna handled the details of the move across the country, the purchase of their new house, and the work of getting it ready. Sandy made sure all of Deanna's questions were answered and helped connect her with a moving company and a handyman.

After Deanna and Becky closed on their new home, Deanna invited Sandy over for lunch. There was an attraction obvious to both of them that neither could ignore. One thing led to another and they had sex on the kitchen floor. Deanna told Sandy she and Becky started having problems shortly after they got married. Becky was emotionally and physically abusive and the two of them had not been intimate for quite some time.

Sandy said she knew what Deanna was going through. Her ex-partner, Pam, also had been emotionally abusive. Sandy had to file a restraining order to break free of her.

Deanna was surprised. She had no idea because Sandy seemed so strong and independent.

They began an affair, and after six months, Sandy asked Deanna to leave Becky and move in with her. Deanna told Becky she wanted a divorce because she was in love with Sandy. Becky spiraled out of control and smashed Deanna's phone against the wall. She also keyed the new Lexus she had given Deanna for her birthday, leaving a long deep scratch along the driver's side.

Initially, things between Sandy and Deanna were amazing, and Sandy was happy to be in a stable and happy relationship. Sandy felt she and Deanna were destined to be together.

But after Becky finally agreed to sign the divorce papers and they reached a financial settlement, Deanna's demeanor began to change. She began picking fights and told Sandy she was becoming too needy when she wanted to talk about their relationship. One night they went to dinner and a guy Sandy knew from high school walked by their table. When Sandy stood up and gave him a big hug and kiss, it did not sit well with Deanna. After he left to go back to his table, Deanna accused Sandy of being way too friendly with the guy. Sandy tried to explain they had known each other since middle school, but Deanna said she didn't want to hear any more bullshit and tossed her plate of food in Sandy's face. Sandy was in shock, stood up from the table, and ran into the bathroom crying. When she came out, Deanna was gone.

That incident was the straw that broke the camel's back. Sandy found my name online and scheduled an appointment, insisting she and Deanna come to therapy together.

When Sandy and Deanna walked into my office, Sandy was eager to talk about the incident that led them to schedule an appointment. She told the story of what had happened at the restaurant, speaking slowly and ever so gingerly while glancing over to Deanna to make sure she was not upsetting her.

When she got to the part where Deanna threw the food in her face, Deanna chimed in, "So this meeting you set up is about attacking me?"

"What about all the things you have done?" Sandy said.

From out of nowhere, Deanna burst into tears and said "Becky and I never had these types of problems in our marriage." As Sandy handed her a tissue, a switch seemed to flip and Deanna continued, "And you are a selfish bitch. Even your friends have warned me about you." Deanna then burst into tears while simultaneously urging Sandy to hold her because she was feeling unloved.

By our fourth session, things were not progressing. Deanna's emotions kept jumping all over the place until finally, toward the end of one of our sessions, she got up and walked out. I asked Sandy if she felt counseling was helping them because it didn't appear we were moving forward.

Sandy asked, "Do you think Deanna has borderline personality disorder? Pam also had it, and I have a feeling I'm back in the same type of relationship with Deanna." Sandy obviously was knowledgeable about BPD.

Deanna walked back in and said she was feeling better. I asked if I could have a few minutes with Deanna alone. When Sandy left, I chose my words carefully and, being mindful of Deanna's body language, told her I was concerned about her emotional instability.

Deanna said, "I am only this way when I'm around Sandy, and even my friends have warned me she is a narcissist."

I responded, "You might disagree but you are showing a lot of emotional fluctuation in our sessions, and—"

Deanna cut me off, "My therapist said I am an empath and I'm only reacting to Sandy's toxic behavior."

I said, "Perhaps you could talk to your therapist about my observations and see what kind of feedback she can offer." I felt it was best to end the conversation there.

Some background information on this couple would be helpful.

Sandy was adopted and her adoptive parents were both narcissistic. Her mother drank excessively and her father beat her mother regularly. Sandy felt like drama followed her everywhere she went, eventually leading to the very toxic relationship she had with Pam.

Deanna insisted she had a wonderful childhood. Sandy reminded her it was important to reveal she was sexually abused by her brother. When she finally got up enough courage to tell her mother about it, her mother responded, "Stop making things up. Your brother is a good boy."

Both Sandy and Deanna had a lot of past trauma and healing that they needed to resolve. Instead, they were attracted to one another hoping for a happy life together. It is difficult to have a healthy relationship if the individuals are not healthy themselves. I have said many times in a session, "Two broken people cannot come together and make a healthy relationship." Your partner should *complement* you, not *complete* you as I mentioned before.

Several months later I was traveling out of town when I got a phone call from Deanna. At first, I didn't connect her with the name until she started talking about Sandy. They had decided to take a break from each other. She wanted to assure me she was not mentally ill and hoped she didn't leave a bad impression on me because she really was a very good-hearted person. I told her I appreciated the call and wished both of them my best.

Clinical Thoughts

I mentioned at the beginning of this book that some relationships are not going to be repaired. In this case, Sandy and Deanna will either remain together in a toxic relationship or separate. Deanna's BPD was apparent, one minute saying her marriage to Becky was healthy and the next minute saying Becky was abusive and controlling. Sandy said she had no idea why she attracted emotionally needy and unstable women.

Clients who have BPD can be challenging. Underneath their mental health condition, they feel overwhelmingly empty inside. As a therapist, I struggle with giving my clinical insight and diagnosis to a person who already feels "less than" and inadequate. I have seen some clients feel a huge sense of relief because they finally understood their behavior. Others have told me they didn't feel I knew them well enough and indicated, without mincing many words, that I was incompetent.

Therapists see a lot of clients who struggle with BPD and their symptoms can vary in severity. From my experience, I have seen a consistent pattern where clients who have a personality disorder attract a partner with a personality disorder. A narcissistic person can only partner with a person who allows them to be narcissistic. An emotionally unstable person, such as someone with BPD, can be the ideal match for a narcissist even though their relationships are often quite toxic. These relationships are built on an unhealthy foundation of insecurity, trauma, and pain.

Therapeutic Advice

In the case of Sandy and Deanna, both had a history of trauma and abuse. They carried their traumas into their adult relationships, first with other partners and then with each other. Emotionally, they attached to each other at a low but intense vibrational frequency.

Dr. David Hawkins developed a scale that measures emotions in Hertz (Hz) to indicate their energy frequency. Emotions range from very low, 20 Hz, to very high, 700-100 Hz. Although you may not be familiar with the term Hertz, you are probably more in tune to vibrational energy and emotions than you realize. When you are with someone who is miserable, you can feel their pain. Misery and shame are heavy, overwhelming, and often exhausting. Jealousy and anger are emotions that have a vibrational frequency of 125 Hz and 150 Hz. These frequencies are still low but very intense. This is where Sandy and Deanna attached to each other on a regular and consistent basis.

On a more positive note, when you are around someone who has high vibrational energy, such as a motivational speaker or an enthusiastic individual, you feel invigorated by their energy because this type of vibrational energy can range from 700-1000 Hz. A high vibrational energy will not attach to a low vibrational energy, particularly in relationships, because the two frequencies are not compatible.

Over time, if our vibrational energy is low because of our fears, worries, guilt, and stress, we will attract other people who attach to us at that level of frequency. An example would be the person at work who thrives on drama and gossip. Her trusty companions are going to be other employees who enjoy gossiping and drama also. Many times, relationships break down because both partners are attached to each other at a low frequency, again apparent in the story of Sandy and Deanna.

The nervous system needs to maintain balance. Because individuals lead stressful lives, the mind becomes extremely active if the nervous system is out of balance. A vibration of 175 Hz and below will cause the body to stress because the emotional frequency at these lower levels is fear-based. Examples are "My biggest fear is…." "I'm so nervous because…." "I worry about….."These types of thought patterns put a tremendous amount of stress on the body because the body cannot decipher whether the thought is real or imagined.

Many times, we look to our partners to help us through feelings of anxiety, stress, depression, and fear. In many cases, such as the death of a child or loss of a job, the partner may experience the same emotion. When both are stretched to the limit, they have nothing left to give each other. When that demand comes, it is often met with anger or withdrawal which ultimately makes the situation worse for both.

> *When you have doubts about your relationship, hit the pause button.*

Chapter 9

The story of Audrey and Kyle

Audrey met Kyle two weeks after she filed a restraining order against her boyfriend Ed. She and Ed had been together for several years, and Ed had a long history of being verbally and emotionally abusive towards Audrey. In time, Ed's explosive rages became physical. One Saturday night, he nearly choked Audrey to the point of unconsciousness. She managed to break free but suffered a dislocated shoulder and two fractured ribs.

After that assault, Audrey left Ed and, moved back in with her parents but hated living under their roof at the age of 29. Lonely and depressed, Audrey decided to get on Tinder to see if she could find a guy to talk to and keep her company. Kyle's profile picture and bio caught her eye. He said he loved the outdoors and wanted someone to go on adventures with him and travel the world. Audrey thought this could be the guy for her.

Things between Audrey and Kyle started like a fairytale. They met at a bar, had a few drinks, and ended their first date at his place where they had sex. Audrey told Kyle she felt instantly attracted to him, and he said the feeling was mutual.

Audrey worked at a doctor's office and the staff were excited for her when Kyle had flowers delivered to the office and surprised her by buying her an occasional lunch. Kyle texted Audrey long, loving messages and she couldn't help but get excited when she saw his name come up on her phone.

Kyle asked Audrey to move in three weeks after they first met and she was more than ready to get out of her parent's house. Audrey's parents had reservations about her becoming involved and moving in with someone she just met, but nothing they could say would change her mind.

Since both worked during the day, they enjoyed spending evenings together. Kyle had two children by two different women with whom he shared joint custody. Kyle said both his children's mothers, he used the term "baby mommas," were "crazy bitches" and he assured Audrey he knew how to deal with both of them. Audrey thought Kyle probably had never found the kind of true love like the kind they had with each other.

But the fairy tale didn't last. One night, Kyle seemed "off" and Audrey wondered what was wrong. He became dismissive and told her to not be so clingy. When she pressed him, he picked her up, put her outside on their porch, and locked her out of the house. Audrey started banging on the door, begging Kyle to let her in. It was nearly 9:00 p.m. and Audrey was still outside, barefoot with no jacket to keep her warm.

When Kyle finally opened the door, almost an hour later, Audrey was hysterical. She said, "Why did you lock me out of the house? What did I do?"

Kyle shrugged his shoulders and said, "It wasn't like I was going to leave you outside all night so what's your problem?"

Although this incident was reminiscent of Audrey's relationship with Ed, she couldn't bear the thought of calling her parents and moving back in with them again. Unfortunately, Kyle started drinking heavily and micromanaged everything she said and did. Kyle refused to let Audrey call or go out with her friends because he was convinced that she would cheat on him if given the chance. He also forbade Audrey to see her parents because he knew they didn't like him. When Audrey came home five minutes late from the grocery store, Kyle accused her of talking to other guys and demanded she tell him the dude's name she was screwing.

One night, Audrey had enough and started packing her things. Kyle began to cry and said he was willing to go to counseling and didn't know why he acted the way he did. Audrey felt bad for him and started looking for therapists. I was the first therapist who called her back.

When Audrey and Kyle came to see me, our session started well. I asked both of them a lot of questions and Kyle appeared relaxed and was cooperative.

When there was a slight break in the conversation, Audrey said, "I don't like it when Kyle calls me names."

"Can you give me an example?" I asked.

"Yes, he calls me a stupid fucking whore when I don't do what he wants," Audrey said and quickly rattled off several more expletives.

Without a change in tone or body language, I said "Kyle, is what Audrey saying true?"

He said, "Yes, she pisses me off and I get tired of her whining and all the other bullshit she does."

"Why do you speak to her that way?" I asked.

Kyle stood up and said, "I've had enough of this shit" and walked out of my office, slamming the door behind him.

In response to his outburst, Audrey said she had a gut feeling early on that she should end it with Kyle. She kept hoping he would change. As she continued talking, she peeked out my office window. Then she said, "I'm relieved that Kyle's car is parked out front. I was hoping I wouldn't need to call an Uber like I did the last time he drove off and left me stranded."

Before Audrey left my office, I had a fifteen-minute heart-to-heart with her. I told her I would likely never see her again, but I wanted her to hear my concerns. I was clear about Kyle's narcissistic/antisocial personality traits and told her it was not likely he would change.

Audrey said she understood and thanked me for caring so much about her.

I watched as Audrey hurried out to their car in a rather submissive posture. I did not expect to see her and Kyle again. As they drove off, I took my mother's advice and gave it to God.

Clinical Thoughts

This case reminded me of one of my favorite Maya Angelou quotes, "When someone shows you who they really are, believe them!"

Audrey has dependent personality disorder which is an overwhelming fear of separation and clinging, needing a lot of reassurance. Unfortunately, people with dependent personality disorder often attract abusive partners.

Audrey's boundaries were poorly defined if, indeed, she had any boundaries at all. If she did, I wasn't clear what they were. She tolerated abuse and told me how much she loved Kyle.

When I asked her what her definition of love, she said, "He had a steady job and helped pay my bills." That was the saddest definition of love I had ever heard.

Although Audrey was lonely and wanted companionship, she didn't give herself the time or space to heal from the past abuse she experienced with Ed. The fact that she tolerated such severe abuse with both Ed and Kyle was an indication Audrey had her own issues that needed to be explored. I was sorry she hadn't considered working with a therapist sooner. Unfortunately, Audrey and Kyle may still be together but therapy would not be helpful for them. Not as long as Kyle is unwilling to change and Audrey is unwilling to set boundaries.

Therapeutic Advice

If you decide to leave a non-working or abusive relationship, it may be easy to recall all the things the other person did to justify leaving them. Yet, more importantly, the work needs to start with healing from within. Even though your partner may have been abusive or toxic, there was also a part of you that allowed, overlooked, and accepted this type of behavior.

In my book Insightful Self-Therapy, I wrote a chapter about setting and enforcing boundaries. I ended the chapter with a "call to action," and I feel my advice is worth repeating.

Get out a piece of paper and make a large circle. Inside the circle, write a few words that describe your values. For example, "Honesty and respect from myself and others." Be honest about your true values. Are they the values you have been living? Would others recognize your description of yourself and agree those are your values?

After you are comfortable with what you have written in your circle, think about whether or not the people and circumstances in your life align with what you have defined as important to you. If you describe yourself as a kind person, spending time around negative friends who enjoy talking badly about others might not be right for you.

Never tolerate being disrespected.

Chapter 10

The story of Frank and Margaret

Frank and Margaret had been married for 38 years and had two adult children who no longer lived at home.

Frank was a retired engineer and Margaret was a retired accountant. During their entire marriage, Frank assumed all the responsibilities for the household including cooking, cleaning, and raising the children. He typically left work around 5:00 p.m. to pick up the children from their after-school activities, feed them dinner, and help them with their homework. Margaret felt no obligation to the family.

This continued year after year until the children graduated high school and went off to college. After college, neither expressed any interest in coming back home for any length of time and both moved out of state after graduation. Frank and Margaret saw the kids as adults but seldom made any effort to interact with them.

During the Covid lockdown, Frank found out that Margaret was having an emotional affair with Doug. Doug was the ex-husband of one of Margaret's co-workers. Margaret had casually mentioned to Frank that Doug and his wife divorced, but since Frank had only met Doug a handful of times, he didn't think much of it.

Margaret's affair took Frank by surprise. Although he had noticed that she was texting frequently, it never occurred to him that she had another man in her life. He only became suspicious when their financial advisor called Frank to see if everything was okay. He told Frank that Margaret had called him out of the blue asking to have $30,000 transferred from her IRA account. The advisor wondered if Frank and Margaret were planning a nice vacation and certainly hoped nothing was wrong.

After doing some digging, Frank discovered that Margaret had already transferred $25,000 into Doug's account over the past year. This did not include the $30,000 he had been called about by their financial advisor. When Frank confronted Margaret about it, Margaret said it was just a loan and Doug would be paying her back. She was perturbed Frank would even question the decisions she made regarding "her"' money! Frank was dumbfounded.

Frank decided to take a look at Margaret's cell phone one afternoon when she was showering and found dozens of exchanges with Frank, calls and texts throughout the day and night. That certainly explained why Margaret had been choosing to sleep in the living room instead of in their bed. And here she had him believing she had hurt her back playing pickleball. When Frank confronted Margaret about the affair, she was ambivalent about directly answering his questions and quickly became dismissive regarding his accusations.

The next thing Frank noticed, Margaret started texting Doug right in front of him. Frank couldn't believe Margaret acted so heartlessly and threw her affair in his face the way she did. Yet, they continued living a "normal" life getting together with friends who had no idea they were having marital difficulties.

Over Thanksgiving, their son, Jason, and daughter-in-law, Monica, came to visit and couldn't help but notice that their mother seemed distracted. When they asked Frank if she was okay, he told the kids the truth. Jason was furious. He stormed into the kitchen and found Margaret pretending to get dinner ready while secretly texting Doug. Her back was to Jason as he made his way through the doorway. Jason screamed at Margaret and told her she had some nerve cheating on his dad. He said he hated her and would not stay in a home with such a selfish, egotistical, cheater of a mother any longer. Monica ran into the bedroom crying hysterically and packed their belongings. Jason apologized to Frank but insisted he and Monica go to a hotel.

Mortified, Margaret grabbed her suitcase and told Frank she was moving out. A few days after she left, Frank pulled up all charges on their joint credit card. Within three days after moving out, he saw that Margaret had charged a very expensive trip to Aruba. Coming to terms that their marriage was over, Frank scheduled a consultation with a divorce attorney and did his best to explain their circumstances to their friends and neighbors while the children remained supportive.

Three weeks later, Margaret called Frank saying she wanted to come back home. Frank agreed with no questions asked, assuming Margaret had learned her lesson and realized "the grass wasn't always greener on the other side." He welcomed Margaret back with open arms, never mentioning the trip to Aruba and all the money missing from their bank account.

Unfortunately, it soon became clear that Margaret did not end her affair with Doug. She told Frank she loved Doug and looked forward to the flirtatious texts he was sending her every morning.

Frank didn't know what to do and decided he needed professional help. He felt that Margaret had no remorse about hurting him or hurting the children, and he was at a loss for what to do next. Frank suggested he and Margaret go to couples counseling. They went to see a therapist twice but Margaret was adamant she would not be going back. Frank scheduled an appointment for individual counseling with me after his primary care physician suggested he find someone to talk to. He had lost fifteen pounds and was in the emergency room twice in one week diagnosed with panic attacks both times.

I met with Frank on a Thursday afternoon. He told his story very matter-of-factly with almost no emotion. There were times when he would laugh nervously even though his story was anything but laughable.

At one point during our sessions, I said, "Frank, how have you been able to tolerate this for so long?"

"I really don't know," he said with his nervous laugh. "I guess I'm just a pathetic person."

I told Frank he could either stay married to Margaret, knowing she was not likely going to change, or choose to end the marriage and move on.

He said, "You have given me a lot to think about."

As Frank walked out of my office, I thought it was doubtful Frank would divorce Margaret, but I couldn't help but feel hopeful he might consider it.

The next day, I had a text from Frank telling me before he had a chance to talk to Margaret about our session, she had moved out again. He had called the children and they were, once again, supportive and understanding. I told him I would be available if he needed anything and thanked him for the update.

A week later, the phone rang and it was Frank. "Oh, hey Denise. I just wanted to give you another update," he said. "Margaret said she wanted to come back so I decided to give her another chance."

"Ok, Frank," I replied. "Thank you for calling."

Clinical Conclusions

Frank suffers from Dependent Personality Disorder (DPD) which we talked about earlier in this book. In graduate school, my professor called such a person a clinging vine. In layman's terms, Frank allows himself to be a doormat and has very poor, even nonexistent, boundaries. I had talked to Frank during one of our sessions about my concerns with him having DPD. All he said after I gave him a lengthy explanation of it was "Yeah, I know."

Working with clients who have such personality disorders is challenging. DPD is difficult because it can be hard to understand why someone would allow another person to mistreat them time after time. In Frank's case, Margaret had neglected him throughout their entire marriage. He said he never stood up to her and felt it was easier to please her than confront her about it. It must have been difficult for their children to be raised in this type of dysfunctional dynamic. Frank said both of his children were angry with their mother, especially when they reached adulthood, and told her how they felt abandoned by her. Jason shared with Frank that Margaret was never a good mother. When Frank told Margaret what their son had said about her, she was shocked and yelled at Frank, calling their son rude and ungrateful. I imagine Frank offered Margaret no input whatsoever.

Although I have never met Frank and Margaret's children, it is likely both of them have been affected by their parent's dysfunctional marriage. Hard as it may seem to imagine, Jason may have married someone very similar to Margaret even though he said he hated her. While children may not like the dynamics of their parent's marriage, they often incorporate them into their behavior. In my experience, children either marry the polar opposite of their parents, as far as their personality is concerned, or they repeat their parents' dysfunctional relationship dynamic.

The sad truth for Frank is if he were to finally divorce Margaret, he would likely end up in the same type of abusive dynamic in his next relationship moving forward. Frank's unhealthy marriage was something he had tolerated for over three decades. Margaret knew the "rules" in their marriage which were "there weren't any rules." Yes, her behavior and the way she treated Frank were unacceptable, but Frank had a choice also. In his marriage, Frank chose to do nothing.

Therapeutic Advice:

Margaret has NPD. If you are in a relationship with a narcissist, you probably feel trapped. But remember, you are not a victim and you do have choices. If you are not willing to get out of the relationship, you must learn to live with your partner and accept things the way they are. Things are not going to change. If you feel like you want or need better for yourself and your children, you have no other choice than to muster the courage to leave.

> *Never text a conversation*
> *that needs to happen in person.*

Chapter 11

The story of Chris and Jessica

Chris and Jessica had lived together for seven years. Chris worked nights and Jessica worked 7 a.m. to 7 p.m. as a cardiac nurse. They would see each other for an hour, on average, like ships passing in the night. As time went on, they began to feel disconnected from each other.

Before Chris left for work, he and Jessica had little if any conversation. Soon after Chris clocked in at the factory, however, the text messages would start:

Jessica: WTF Chris? Why couldn't you get up an hour earlier and start the laundry?

Chris: IDK—I don't know! What's the big deal?

Jessica: The big deal is that you don't respect me. You think I have nothing else to do at night other than the laundry, take care of the dog and meal prep. I don't know why you treat me like crap all the time. You don't give a shit about anyone but yourself. I am a NURSE and I take care of sick people all day long. I already have a lot of responsibility. You just don't get it.

Chris: Okay, Jess. Really? I don't respect you? WTF is wrong with you? You are so selfish and, by the way, I KNOW you are a NURSE. I'm the one who paid for half of your nursing school. As far as the dog is concerned, I know he needs his medications. I don't need you to treat me like a child and leave me notes and reminders. Honestly, you are pathetic sometimes.

Jessica: Ok, put all our problems on me. Fine. You are perfect, Chris, and you don't have any flaws. I'm the one who is fucked up. There! Are you happy now?

Chris: I'm done having this conversation with you. I'm busy at work. How about you bother someone else now.

Jessica: You are pathetic.

I had been seeing Jessica for individual counseling for two years but this was the first time she shared these types of text exchanges she had with Chris. Jessica said they had a lot of issues but the primary problem was they didn't know how to communicate. Jessica read a few more of the text message exchanges out loud in session, hoping I would take her side and agree that Chris was a jerk.

"Can I ask you a question, Jess?" I said. "Do you feel it is helping your relationship to have these conversations over text?"

"No, I guess not but we never have time to talk so he needs to know how I feel."

"I agree," I said. "But certain feelings and conversations need to take place either in person or in front of a counselor if you feel neither of you can have a civil conversation together."

My sessions with Jessica felt like we were on a merry-go-round. Both she and Chris were addicted to their back-and-forth texting drama, yet frustrated that they could never get past their issues of not feeling respected and valued by each other.

I suggested Jessica ask Chris if he would consider coming in with her for a session together. When I opened my office door for our next scheduled appointment, I was surprised to see them both standing there.

Jessica and Chris were open about expressing their concerns about each other and the impact it has had on their relationship. Jessica said she felt they had been disconnected for a long time but she did love Chris and they both wanted to learn helpful tools to be able to communicate better. After several sessions together, during which I gave them suggestions on what to do, Jessica and Chris said they felt therapy was helpful and said they would call when they were ready for another session.

Six weeks later, I was pleased to see Jessica's name on my schedule for a follow-up meeting. This time she came in alone and said the counseling sessions she and Chris had together made a huge difference in their relationship. They were practicing the tools we talked about and felt they were heading in the right direction. Jessica said although they have had a few minor incidents, they were happier than they had been in a long time.

Clinical Thoughts

Communication is the number one issue I hear couples offer as the biggest obstacle in their relationship. If verbal communication is challenging, imagine how hard it is to navigate a relationship over text.

Communication is not conveyed with words alone. Tone, timing, and delivery are essential to understand and be understood. In the book *The 7 Habits of Highly Effective People*

Stephen Covey talks about six key factors needed for building relationships:

- Understanding the individual—it can be hard to address the concerns or feelings of another person when you haven't taken the time to understand what they are.

- Attending to the little things—respect, being on time, and practicing thoughtfulness.

- Clarifying expectations—particularly with roles and goals.

- Showing personal integrity—being honest, resisting the need to gossip about others.

- Apologizing Sincerely—recognizing when you have failed to do something or disappointed someone and sincerely apologizing. Overusing the word "I'm sorry" will cause those words to not feel genuine.

While communication among couples can be difficult, social media and discussing problems over text make it worse. On the one hand, it allows people to go over the top because they don't have to experience the immediate effects; on the other, it limits their experience and practice of genuine face-to-face contact, with spouses, family, and friends.

When articulating feelings, experiences, perceptions, and/or emotions, it is extremely important to incorporate tone, understanding, and the effectiveness of your overall approach or delivery. When engaging in conversation be mindful of words and the perception of those words to your partner.

Therapeutic Advice

I had a few communication guidelines I offer which have proved to be fairly effective for couples who are invested in improving their relationship:

- Text messages should be brief and not used to communicate relationship issues.

- Take into account the personalities and values of your partner. For example, a husband will take the garbage if asked but may not notice the garbage is overflowing on his own.

- Always be respectful when communicating. Never curse or swear at your partner.

- Remember that your partner is somebody that you love and don't assume your partner can read your mind. Ask for what you want or need politely.

- If you complain about everything, your partner is more likely to ignore the constant harassment. Choose your battles and learn to tolerate honest differences of opinion.

- Acknowledge the things your partner does that you like. For example, thank you for doing the laundry.

- Make time for each other. For example, date night. Be present and actively listen to each other.

- When spending time together, put away cell phones and have conversations with each other. Resist walking away and putting away the dishes while your partner is talking to you.

- Communicate the feelings beneath anger and resentment. For example, I'm overwhelmed, I'm frustrated, I'm disappointed.
- Use language like "when you _____, I feel_____."

One morning, driving to work, I passed a street corner where twelve or so teens were waiting for the school bus. Without exception, they were bent over their phones, texting, playing computer games, etc. Society has never been as connected as we are today. Yet, people are becoming more isolated and increasingly lonely. Human beings thrive on face-to-face connection. This energy exchange cannot be duplicated over a device.

Why your partner's adult children matter.

Chapter 12

The story of
Joyce and Les

Joyce and Les were in their mid-70s and had been married for five years. Joyce was a retired executive, divorced with two adult boys, and Les was a widower with an adult daughter.

When Joyce decided to go on *Match.com*, she was looking for a companion to spend time with, go out to dinner, and travel together. She was perfectly happy being single and had done very well in her career financially. But when she met Les, they had an instant connection.

Les worked on Wall Street in NYC for most of his life. He and his late wife, Pat, had been high school sweethearts and lived outside the city in New Jersey where they raised their daughter and lived a happy life. Eight years ago, Pat lost her life to an aggressive type of colon cancer, less than six months after her initial diagnosis. Les was her primary caretaker until she went to hospice toward the end.

After Pat died, Les was lonely. He felt like a third wheel when he got together with other couples and was tired of eating at home alone. He was hoping to find someone to live the rest of his life with. When Les read Joyce's profile on *Match.com*, she checked every box on his list and then some.

Les and Joyce dated only nine months before they got married. They both owned homes and felt it was important to start a new life together in Florida. Joyce sold her house soon after she put it on the market, but Les dragged his feet about putting a "for sale" sign up on his. Instead, he convinced Joyce to go to New York and spend six weeks there in the summer.

Joyce felt awkward there because Les' adult daughter, Jenny, would join them, set up her work computer in her old room, and act as though she were home from college. Her bedroom looked like a teenager's, with clothes sprawled all over the floor and dirty dishes and empty glasses on her bedside table. Her bathroom was disgusting.

Joyce felt Jenny was a spoiled, thirty-three-year-old brat. Whenever she was upset or "needed" her father, she called or texted him incessantly. If he didn't respond right away, Jenny yelled at Les, accusing him of neglecting her. Les felt guilty because Jenny no longer had a mother. Joyce was annoyed that Les answered Jenny's calls regardless of what time of day or night they came in.

Joyce found my name online and made an appointment for herself. An hour before her scheduled session, she texted to ask if she could bring Les with her. I texted her back and said I was looking forward to meeting them both.

Joyce and Les were a delightful couple and seemed to get along well. Joyce started by sharing how she had met Les, sold her house in Chattanooga, and built a home together in a 55+ community perfect for their active lifestyle. Les wanted me to know about Pat. He had read I was a nurse and thought I would understand all he had been through. Both were curious as to why I had decided to become a therapist after so many years of working with the critically ill. It is a common question I get asked. I shared how I loved nursing but the 12-hour shifts and being on call became increasingly taxing as I got older. Yet, I loved helping people and went back to school to become a therapist a decade ago. It was one of the best decisions I had ever made.

It wasn't too far into our session when Joyce began addressing her concerns with Jenny. She said if it weren't for her, she and Les wouldn't need marriage counseling. Joyce felt Les acted more like Jenny's husband than her father. While Joyce realized that Jenny was single, in her 30s, and had lost her mother, her attachment to Les didn't feel healthy or appropriate. Joyce was also upset that Les had made no effort whatsoever to sell their family home in New Jersey. She was tired of hearing all of his excuses.

Joyce said, "Denise, have you ever heard of pillow talk?"

"Yes," I said, feeling every bit of my age knowing the term.

"One night during pillow talk, Les confessed he had not sold the house because Jenny couldn't bear the thought of leaving her childhood home," Joyce continued. "I have never heard such ridiculous nonsense."

Les chimed in, "Jenny has been through a lot, losing her mother, and I don't want to do anything to upset her."

I said, "It seems Jenny relies on you to help her navigate her life as well as her emotions."

"Exactly right", Joyce confirmed. "You just say it a lot nicer than I do."

I spent the majority of our sessions helping Les understand that it was not his job to make sure Jenny was okay. It was important for her, for everyone in fact, to learn how to take care of their own emotions.

Joyce said Les needed to make a choice. He could either be married to Jenny or to her.

"Do you want to stay married to Joyce?" I asked Les.

"More than anything" he answered without hesitation.

We practiced role-playing scenarios to help Les interact with his daughter more appropriately.

Les and Joyce gave examples of Jenny's outrageous behavior and I gave Les the tools and language to navigate through it. I emphasized the importance of being kind, respectful, and clear with Jenny but also assured them it was not going to be easy. Jenny's controlling and manipulative behavior had been working well for her for a very long time. I encouraged Les to resist parenting Jenny from a place of guilt and fear.

Joyce, Les, and I met for a total of three sessions. Toward the end, Joyce was pleased to tell me that things were going well. The first few weeks of "The New Les" were tough for Jenny. She was like a five-year-old in a 33-year-old's body, which caused Les a lot of anxiety. But, to his credit, he stayed kind, clear, and respectful with Jenny.

Les commented he had written himself a note on a piece of paper and kept it in his wallet. He had written "WWDD" which stood for "What would Denise do?" I chuckled at the thought of making one of those "WWDD" pieces of paper for my husband too.

Les sold his home in New Jersey and donated all of his late wife's belongings to charity. Jenny said she understood her father wanted to create a new life with Joyce but did have a meltdown when the "sold" sign went up in the yard.

Clinical Thoughts

Shortly after I went into practice, I had a similar case. At that time, I was still an intern and asked my supervisor if she had any suggestions I hadn't thought of. She said, "Ah yes, your client needs to wean her adult daughter off her breast." I was a bit taken aback by her directness but later thought she made a very good point.

When couples come in for counseling, it is important for them to stay open-minded and willing to do something different. If you think about it, it is the only way to solve a problem. To solve a problem, you need to do something different. As Albert Einstein famously said, "Insanity is doing the same thing over and over again and expecting different results."

In this case, Les was ready and willing to learn more effective skills to set limits with Jenny. I also credit Joyce for putting her foot down and finding a therapist, a neutral party, to help them.

In the end, Jenny learned to take responsibility for her happiness. At Les' suggestion, she found a therapist to help her and started going to counseling weekly.

According to Les, it made all the difference in the world. "It has been great knowing she can bitch about her life to her therapist and not me!" he said.

I said I was glad she found someone to talk to.

Therapeutic advice:

Parents should not wait until children are grown to teach them to be self-sufficient and to take responsibility for themselves. The longer you wait, the more difficult it can be for the children to learn these skills. The process should begin in early childhood.

A few examples of teaching self-sufficiency and responsibility include:

- Chores of increasing difficulty as the child ages and matures.

- Helping children learn the value of money by requiring them to earn and manage a modest allowance.

- Setting firm limits and boundaries.

- Communicating clearly and effectively.

- Teaching children there are consequences to every choice they make, be they good or bad.

With regard to a blended family, here are some thoughts and guidelines to consider:

- Children must respect the new dynamic of the relationship. This does not mean that the parent would love the children any less, but rather the children shouldn't dominate the new paradigm.

- As far as stepchildren, the biological parent should handle parenting matters, including discipline if necessary.

- It is very important for the newly joined couple to have a discussion early in their relationship about their expectations regarding the children.

- That same discussion should be communicated to the children about expectations that include them.

Love after your partner has departed.

Chapter 13

The story of Elaine and Howard

After more than 40 years of marriage, Elaine couldn't believe that Richard was suddenly gone. They had just booked a cruise to the Caribbean when he started complaining of indigestion. Two days later, Elaine found Richard on the bathroom floor dead of a heart attack.

Six months later, Elaine still felt overwhelmed by grief. Everything she tried to accomplish seemed impossible. She had no idea how to live. A caring neighbor, who had been widowed for several years, encouraged her to join a support group and recommended *GriefShare*. Not familiar with the program, Elaine went online to read more.

A *GriefShare* support group is a safe, welcoming place where people understand the difficult emotions of grief. Through this 13-week group, you'll discover what to expect in the days ahead and what's "normal" in grief. Since there are no neat, orderly stages of grief, you'll learn helpful ways of coping with grief, in all its unpredictability—and gain solid support each step of the way.

The description spoke to Elaine's feelings, and she signed up for the program. She hoped the group sessions would help her find a new approach to coping with her loss, but it was several weeks before she got up the courage to go to a meeting.

As the group leader went around the room, asking everyone to introduce themselves and tell the participants whom they had lost, Elaine couldn't hold back her tears.

When it was her turn, she said "I'm Elaine McDermott and I lost my husband Richard of 46 years to a heart attack." She couldn't get out another word.

Fortunately, the man next to her took over. "Hello everyone, my name is Howard, and I lost my wife of 49 years to breast cancer," he said. "I am here because I need to move forward with my life. My children are worried about me and I don't want to be a burden to them. I'm glad to meet all of you and thank you for listening."

For the next session, Elaine sat next to Howard. She felt comfortable knowing he was there even though they hardly spoke to each other. At the end of their eighth meeting, the group leader invited Elaine to stay for coffee. Reluctantly, Elaine agreed and sat by Howard. As they struck up a conversation, Elaine was surprised to learn they had grown up "next door" from each other in two adjacent suburbs outside of Cleveland. Before long, Elaine and Howard developed a wonderful friendship and started meeting regularly for breakfast.

A year went by and Elaine and Howard became romantically involved. It felt awkward and nice at the same time. They started telling friends and family they were officially dating. Both sets of children supported their relationship. When they got married, Elaine and Howard had a small, intimate wedding, with only their families attending.

Although Elaine and Howard were happy together, Elaine felt guilty about remarrying. She didn't think she had the right to fully enjoy herself because Richard had died and never got to live out his life Not knowing how to help Elaine through the guilt, Howard suggested she talk to someone.

I saw Elaine on a Monday afternoon. She sat down and started in immediately, "I would like you to know why I'm here and what happened to my Richard."

I have learned when clients are eager to tell their stories, it is best place to let them take the lead.

Elaine went into great detail about Richard—how they met, what kind of work he did, the children they had together, and how he died. When people experience a tragic event, they often remember every detail. Elaine was no exception. She told me what she was cooking for breakfast the morning she found Richard dead in the bathroom, whom she called for help, and how the paramedics comforted her, word-for-word, when they arrived on the scene.

Halfway through the session, Elaine mentioned *GriefShare* and how she met Howard. I noted that she was careful and deliberate, letting me know that dating and marrying Howard had been a slow process.

Elaine's struggle with her feelings of guilt was not uncommon. After a few sessions, I asked her how she would have felt if she had died on the bathroom floor and Richard was left a widower. "Would you be okay if Richard were to find a companion then?"

"Oh yes," she said. "Richard couldn't do his own laundry or cook a meal, he would have needed someone to take care of him."

"Would you want him to feel guilty for that?"

"No." Elaine thought for a moment and continued, "Now that you put it that way, I see your point."

It took a few more sessions, but gradually Elaine's guilt began to lift. I was thrilled to hear that she and Howard booked a cruise to the Caribbean especially since it was a trip she had planned on taking with Richard.

After telling me their plans, she said "Richard knew how much I had been looking forward to visiting the Caribbean and he would be happy knowing I'm finally getting there."

Clinical Thoughts

It's not unusual to feel grief-stricken and suffer from "survivor's guilt" for some time. There are situations where the surviving spouse dies soon after their partner passes. The medical term for this is takosubo syndrome or broken heart syndrome. In any case, grief is a heavy emotion and can wreak havoc on the body too if it is not dealt with and processed appropriately.

The U.S. military has done studies on the most stressful events for soldiers. War and death of a loved one top the list, followed by divorce or separation and moving. In many cases, physical trauma, like aftershocks from an earthquake, occurs within a year.

For many surviving spouses, certain anniversaries or events trigger powerful and painful memories. In time, most people recover and begin to enjoy the "new" normal of their lives. However, a few get stuck. Although antidepressants are not typically the first option of treatment, they can be effective in some cases. People who need medication should not feel ashamed or guilty for asking for help and following the advice and treatment of a qualified practitioner.

To clarify, a therapist (Licensed Psychologist, Licensed Mental Health Counselor, Licensed Clinical Social Worker) provides "talk" therapy, support, and counseling. If medication is indicated, patients are referred to a psychiatrist. Many primary care doctors also may feel comfortable prescribing such medications. I would prefer to refer patients to psychiatrists because their specialty is in mental health.

Therapeutic Advice

We should not stop living our lives because we feel guilty that others are not able to live theirs. Of course, we are going to grieve. It would be abnormal when someone touches your heart and soul not to feel sadness and pain when they die. The "normal" grieving process give or take is six months, on average, but everyone experiences grief differently. Six months is a guideline for therapists to use to help them determine the client's condition, plan, and treatment of care. I usually do not recommend clients begin taking medication before six months but it depends on the individual. Although the grief process is painful, it needs to be experienced. There are always other variables to be considered and recommendations should be made on a case-by-case basis.

A few suggestions to consider when healing from grief:

- Allow the grief to bubble up and be expressed. This may feel embarrassing depending upon when it does, but your friends and family will support you and be okay.

- Eat healthy meals and drink lots of water. When people grieve, they often feel they don't have the energy to eat. It's important to eat something, even if it is a small meal, and make sure you have food regularly.

- Take a nap or go to bed early if you feel exhausted.

- Don't feel like you need to attend every event or disappoint someone by not attending every gathering or answering every call or text. At the same time, be careful not to isolate either. Strike a balance between the two.

- Work with a therapist even if it is short-term. You need someone to help you process the grief appropriately. A therapist can guide you along the way.

- *GriefShare* is one of many support groups. Most towns in The United States offer a support group through hospice. Consider attending such a group.

*The challenges of loving
an older partner.*

Chapter 14

The story of
Emily and Ethan

Emily was only 27 when she and Caleb decided to end their marriage of only two years after Caleb began seeing someone else. Although Emily was devastated, she had checked out of the relationship for some time as well.

Fortunately, they had an amicable divorce, splitting their assets down the middle and going their separate ways. Caleb agreed to take their dog, which was a relief because Emily worked long hours as a commercial realtor, and she was not a dog person anyway.

Because of her successful career, Emily was able to buy a house and a cute little BMW sports car after the divorce. Soon, Emily's work group of friends started offering to fix her up with available guys. However, Emily was not interested. She was busy decorating her new house, going out with other friends, and working.

There was one man on Emily's team she had known for years. Ethan had just turned 40 and was living with his girlfriend Deb. Emily had confided in him going through her separation and divorce, and he had been her voice of reason. Ethan had divorced his wife five years ago shortly after they had a child. He and Emily shared inside jokes, loved the same sports teams, and often quoted lines from their favorite movies with each other during stressful times at work.

Emily considered Ethan a colleague and a good friend. He had known Deb since high school and they seemed very happy. She had no romantic feelings for him but noticed she missed him when he was out of the office or on vacation.

A few weeks after her thirtieth birthday, Emily and Ethan were sitting in the conference room eating lunch. Ethan told Emily that Deb had moved out. Emily was surprised. She said she hadn't realized Deb and Ethan had been unhappy.

Ethan said, "It wasn't exactly that we were unhappy, Deb said it was obvious I would be happier if I were with you!" Emily felt her stomach quiver.

Without another word, they kissed. That first kiss led to a whirlwind romance. Because they were already great friends, sex and intimacy felt natural. They married five years later, just shy of Ethan's 50th birthday. Ethan said he never imagined he would be so happy at fifty.

Twenty years flew by in a flash, and Emily gave Ethan a surprise 70th birthday: a trip to Italy. During their time abroad, Emily noticed a lot of things about Ethan she hadn't seen before. After all, she was still working long hours while Ethan had been retired for almost five years. What concerned her most was his lack of energy and stamina.

When they got home, Emily took the day off to go with Ethan to his doctor's appointment. He had scheduled his annual physical before they left but had not been back to discuss his test results. Emily had hoped the iron supplements Ethan had started taking might be helping.

When Dr. Gray came into the examination room, he apologized and said "Ethan, I'm afraid I have some bad news for you. Your test results are back and you have leukemia. I would like to refer you to an Oncologist and I have already faxed a referral over for you to be seen right away."

Emily and Ethan looked at each other in shock. Not that it is ever a good time for a cancer diagnosis, but she was in the middle of a very busy month. Her mind began to race about all her deadlines that needed to be met until she came to terms and realized that nothing in her life was more important than Ethan and being there for him.

The next several months were spent going from one appointment to another, leading to CT scans, bone scans and ultimately Ethan having several rounds of chemotherapy. The physical toll was difficult on Ethan. The psychological impact and stress was difficult on them both. Ethan felt like he couldn't handle one more appointment when one of his physicians recommended that he see a therapist, but he was supportive when Emily decided she wanted to get help.

When Emily walked into my office, she looked haggard. She said she had been up most of the night before with Ethan who was nauseous and running a low-grade fever. "This is our life now, I'm afraid," she said. "To be honest, I feel selfish admitting to you that I am feeling sorry for myself."

I explained to Emily that when I was an ICU nurse, we were concerned with the caregivers because they suffered as much as the patients.

"I know I would be okay financially if Ethan doesn't make this but I miss my husband and I miss our life" Emily said. "He was always the person I could bounce ideas off, my best friend, my rock." She paused, looked down, and burst into tears.

I wondered if this was the first time she had ever allowed her mind to take her to consider her life without Ethan.

"I hope I don't sound self-centered but I don't want to do this anymore," Emily whispered.

I encouraged her to make time for herself. It was important she remained healthy and to get back to engaging in the things in life she enjoyed. She took my advice and began booking monthly massages and agreed to try acupuncture. She also blocked off her schedule for an hour each morning to get to the gym, asking her brother-in-law to take Ethan for his chemo treatments. He had offered, on many occasions, to help out.

Thankfully, Ethan went into remission last month and he slowly started regaining his strength.

Emily continued coming to counseling on a monthly basis because, as she put it, "Our lives will likely never get back to when we were both working hard and closing deals. I am doing my best to adjust to my new life".

I added. "You are doing a great job!"

Clinical Conclusion

Emily's diagnosis is "adjustment disorder with mixed anxiety and depression," feelings that often go hand-in-hand when an unexpected bump in the road triggers them. In Emily's case, asking for outside help was very wise. Although I'm sure Emily's friends, family, and co-workers supported her, she needed a safe place to process all that went along with Ethan's diagnosis as well as for her health and well-being.

It is not unusual for many happily married couples to have a 10+ year or more age difference. At the beginning of the marriage, when they are younger, they may foresee many challenges but think they'll handle them with ease. Yet, if the older spouse gets sick or just ages naturally, that 10+ age gap may be difficult.

Most of the cases I have seen have involved younger women who are married to older men. While the wife may not have felt the age gap when she was in her thirties to a husband in his forties or fifties, it can be a whole new ballgame ten to twenty years down the road. The thirty-year-old wife married to her husband at forty-five may feel differently when she is sixty-five and he is eighty, particularly if she is in good health and active and he is ailing.

Therapeutic Advice

It is not selfish to begin to create a life separate from your spouse. In the case of my sixty-five-year-old client, she started taking weekend trips with her girlfriends.

When your partner is significantly older, remember they are at a different stage in life than you are. Adjustments need to be made. Otherwise, resentment and bitterness can creep into the relationship.

In the case of Emily, Ethan's medical issues impacted her greatly. This type of overwhelming stress can lead to health problems for the caregivers as well and earlier death if they can't figure out how to keep their life in balance.

Therefore, it is essential to take care of yourself, and it's ok to make yourself a priority. Exercising, eating healthy meals, and drinking plenty of water are just a few necessities. Also, if you have an underlying condition such as high blood pressure or diabetes, make sure you schedule an appointment to check in with your doctor.

Among helpful resources to consider, Deborah Cornwall's book, *Things I Wish I Had Known: Cancer Caregivers Speak Out*, has chapters on "Getting Inside the Caregiver Role" and "Managing Your Emotions and Health."

I encourage anyone going through this type of situation to consider working with a therapist. A therapist can help you look at your situation more objectively and point out things you may have overlooked. I would be happy to help also and you can contact me at *deniseschonwald.com.*

Closing Thoughts

Perhaps the most important realization, which can be a bitter pill to swallow, is one's role in a relationship that isn't working. It's easier to blame a partner, but in the long run that approach is counterproductive.

Most people are not aware of childhood or early experiential trauma and their impact on day-to-day life. Or that they bring them to their relationships. Unresolved, they lead to repetition and you find yourself attracted to people who trigger those responses in you. Unless you deal with them—make changes within yourself—you're more likely to live like the Bill Murray character in the movie *Groundhog Day*.

Not all help needs to be in-depth exploration. Sometimes a few meetings with a counselor can relieve stress and resolve matters. But some situations require considerably more work.

So, I would like to share some "food for thought" or suggestions for you to incorporate into your own life. As I mentioned at the beginning of this book, I highly recommend everyone consider working with a therapist regularly or even now and then. How do you find a good therapist? A good therapist is someone you feel you can connect to.

I suggest you find a therapist who is licensed and one who has completed the education to give you appropriate guidance and treatment. Mental health is a science and its comprehensiveness and expertise cannot be acquired by taking a few courses or classes. I have nine years of education and over thirty years of experience and I am still learning.

One of the ways I continue to learn is by reading books and articles. I am currently re-reading *The Four Agreements* by Don Miguel Ruiz for the third or fourth time. Here is a quote from I wanted to share. If you haven't read this book, it is a must in my opinion:

> *If someone is not treating you with love and respect, it is a gift if they walk away from you. If that person doesn't walk away, you will surely endure many years of suffering with him or her. Walking away may hurt for a while, but your heart will eventually heal. Then you can choose what you really want. You will find that you don't need to trust others as much as you need to trust yourself to make the right choices.*

This section of *The Four Agreements* says it all. Waiting and hoping for people or things to change will only prolong your suffering. You need to take responsibility to create the changes you want in your life based on your beliefs and values. If you don't value yourself, why would anyone else value you?

If you want to enjoy the richness and benefits of a healthy relationship, you need to invest in your health and well-being. Many have said they don't have the time. Yet, the truth is you will either invest in your health or your illness. The same is true of relationships. Relationships are an investment and they take constant work.

I encourage you to do the work. The benefit will be a happy life in a healthy relationship that can potentially be passed down from generation to generation. Give yourself this precious gift.

Please read, learn, and feel free to reach out to me if you have any questions via my website, *deniseschonwald.com.* You also can take a free, ten-question quiz there to learn more about your mental health.

If you are a podcast listener, I have had the honor to be a guest on several podcasts. All the episodes are available at *deniseschonwald.com.*

I look forward to connecting with you.

Acknowledgments

When I decided to write *Elephants Don't Marry Giraffes,* I took common problems I see when working with couples and created stories around them. In one of them, Chapter 7, the story of Sarah, the ending is true.

Dr. Heather Schramm was a remarkable woman, mother, daughter, sister, doctor, and a friend of mine. She was a pediatrician who worked in the suite next to ours. On August 31, 2019, I learned her husband had forced his way into her house and shot her before committing suicide. Her teenage children were hiding in the closet.

Heather was forty-three years old and had recently separated from him. Unfortunately, she didn't live long enough to enjoy the rest of her life and see her children grow up into adults. I miss her dearly and I felt her story needed to be told. I hope it helps someone else. She would have wanted it no other way.

I want to thank Chris Angermann, who helped me edit and publish this book, doing an excellent job of keeping me on track. For some reason, it was challenging for me to write, and I could have easily have pushed it to the side if he hadn't encouraged me to keep at it.

I would also like to thank the many friends who are my biggest cheerleaders. I look up to each and every one of you and am grateful to be in your lives.

Thank you to Nicole Rodrigues and Cindy Cunningham who work diligently to keep my practice running smoothly. They take a lot of the workload off my shoulders so I can write and enjoy practicing.

I am grateful for my children and grandchildren, who are my greatest gifts.

Lastly, a shout-out to my husband Harvey who gives me the time and space to do so many things I enjoy. Thank you, dear.

About Denise

In her more than 30 years working as a registered nurse (BSRN) within the intensive care unit, Denise Schonwald cared for patients who were very ill and often in critical condition. She saw her patients and their families struggling with stress, anxiety, guilt, and fear. She, too, was affected by this challenging environment. To help her clients—and herself—cope, Denise learned various techniques to support mental and emotional well-being. Her success in treating the whole person led her to her calling as a spiritually based licensed mental health counselor and mental intuitive (LMHC). By integrating mental health and physical health into a cohesive treatment plan, Denise provides a holistic approach to her patients. These synergistic treatment methodologies support client healing more effectively than traditional counseling.

Denise has expertise in helping clients through a variety of mental and emotional struggles, including anxiety, depression, panic, marital problems, adolescent behavior issues, family issues, childhood trauma, and more. To assist in her method, she draws upon some rather unconventional sources, including Max, a certified therapy dog, who practiced with her until his passing in June of 2020. Henry, his spirited successor, is now her partner in practice. Additional sources of inspiration include physical activity and various forms of meditation, which help relieve stress and provide mental clarity.

Denise personally enjoys boxing, tennis, and yoga, balancing the physical exercise with meditation, Reiki, and aromatherapy to help integrate physical, mental, and spiritual well-being. Understanding the connection between the mind, body, and spirit, Denise helps clients to explore each avenue to achieve optimum levels of health and wellness.

In addition to working with individuals and families, Denise also supports the wider community through speaking engagements and lectures nationwide. Consider having her speak at your next event and contact her office today.